UNITED METHODISM IN THEORY AND PRACTICE

UNITED METHODISM IN THEORY AND PRACTICE

Roy H. Short

Nashville - ABINGDON PRESS - New York

UNITED METHODISM IN THEORY AND PRACTICE

Copyright © 1974 by Abingdon Press

Library of Congress Cataloging in Publication Data

ISBN 0-687-43009-7

Short, Roy Hunter, Bp., 1902-
    United Methodism in theory and practice.
    1. United Methodist Church (United States)—Govern-
ment. I. Title.
    BX8388.843   262'.07'6   74-13016

MANUFACTURED BY THE PARTHENON PRESS AT
NASHVILLE, TENNESSEE, UNITED STATES OF AMERICA

Contents

I

United Methodism and Method

The United Methodist Church represents one of the largest, strongest, most widely distributed churches of the Christian world, and yet, it is at the same time one of the youngest of the great ecclesiastical bodies.

Its history spans only the last two centuries while some other major denominations were in existence for hundreds of years before it was born.

It is no accident that the development and growth of United Methodism across the years has been what it has.

A Message

One of the secrets of this growth and development was the heralding of a message which the world was eager to hear, a message of redemption and hope for all people everywhere and of challenge to a better way of life for individuals and society. Early Methodism made formal claim to the possession of such a message when it affirmed in its organizing conference in 1784 that its mission was "to reform the Continent and to spread scriptural Holiness over these Lands."

A Passion

Another secret of growth was that the churches which made up United Methodism had a passion, an eager longing to see persons experience the fullness of God's redemption and witness the establishment of the kingdom upon the earth. This passion carried these churches over land and sea, preaching, singing, witnessing, teaching, healing, and ministering with gladness and fervor.

A Method

It must never be forgotten, however, that still another most important secret of the development and growth of United Methodism has been its polity. It has had a message. It has had a mission. But it has also had a method. And by the use of this method it has published the message and given expression to its passion, and made its mission effective.

John Wesley, the founder of Methodism, recognized, as have few men in all ecclesiastical history, the importance of and the possible contribution of method. He preached tirelessly and with magnetic and persuasive power, and multitudes were converted and built up in the faith under his preaching. Also in an effort to reach the unreached and establish converts in the faith, he engaged in the publication of religious literature. He wrote continually, himself, and published much of his writing, including especially his sermons and his significant *Explanatory Notes upon the New Testament*. The world marveled, and still marvels, at the steady stream of works that flowed from his gifted pen especially in light of the fact that he lived so constantly upon the road. His publication supplemented his preaching, stimulated thinking, and challenged response.

But in addition to his relentless preaching and writing, Wesley also gave large and constant attention to method and designing ways and means to preserve the results of his labors. The lay ministry, the provision for classes and bands, and the itinerant system were all designed to conserve the results of the Wesleyan Revival, and ultimately they contributed to its extension across the long years and far beyond the shores of Wesley's beloved England.

The followers of Wesley as dutiful sons have likewise given large attention to method and polity. It has ever been something of a major theme with them, until some persons of other religious persuasions have occasionally accused them of being only activists with an overemphasis upon organization and activity and an insufficient emphasis upon theology.

The followers of Philip William Otterbein in the United Brethren Church and Jacob Albright in the Evangelical Association were characterized by similar attention to method, and parallels in polity development in the Evangelical United Brethren tradition and the Methodist tradition were so common that final union between the two churches in 1968 presented few serious complications.

Changing Method

It should be insisted, however, that United Methodism has never been interested in method simply for method's sake. It has maintained its basic structure, but it has never regarded any feature of its polity as sacrosanct. It has gone upon the assumption that the demands of the mission should determine the method, and it has made countless polity alterations as the years have come and passed.) Each succeeding General Conference has made its own full quota of alterations in the law of the church, and in some cases these alterations have been most far reaching as in the case of: the General Conference of 1808 when a delegated General Conference was first provided for; or the General Conference of 1866 of the Methodist Episcopal Church, South, when the Southern church, which had been so sorely depleted by the war, was set upon an entirely new course; or the General Conference of 1872 of the Methodist Episcopal Church when provision was made for lay representation in the General Conference, as it had been made in the Church, South, six years before.

Other far-reaching changes in polity were made particularly in the Uniting Conference of 1939 which formed The Methodist Church, the Uniting Conference of 1946 which formed the Evangelical United Brethren Church, and the Uniting Conference of 1968 which formed The United Methodist Church.

Other General Conferences in recent years in which more or less radical changes were made in polity, particularly in the realm of board structure, were the 1952 General Conference of The Methodist Church and the 1972 General Conference of The United Methodist Church.

It is well to keep in mind, as the church lives with change, that there has always been some underlying reason for each feature of United Methodist polity as it has developed across the years and as it exists at the moment. The original reason for some particular feature of polity may now be generally forgotten, having become lost in the mists of years long gone. Or conceivably the conditions which originally gave birth to a particular polity feature may no longer exist, and therefore there is no warrant for its continuance. Nevertheless, for United Methodist polity as a whole, there are reasons which still stand and which need therefore to be fully understood. To ferret out the underlying reasons for various features of United Methodist polity is not only to trace an interesting and fascinating story, it is much more—to be put in better position to understand and evaluate adequately United Methodist structure today.

II

The Concept of Connectionalism

The primary mark of United Methodism as a church is that it is a connection. It is not, like the congregational bodies, an association of local churches which choose to relate to each other. Neither is it like the Roman Church subject to a hierarchy finding its summit in a single individual possessed of maximum authority. Nor is it like churches of the Presbyterian order, something of a balance between congregationalism and final responsibility to an overall ecclesiastical body.

Rather it is a unity of which the respective Jurisdictional, Central, and Annual conferences and the various local churches are only local manifestations.

The use of the word "connection" to describe United Methodism goes back to the days of John Wesley. Original Methodism was simply the sum total of those classes, class members, and lay preachers who had chosen to associate themselves with Wesley. In a very real sense he was himself the connection, and while he conferred regularly and respectfully with his associates, he alone made all final decisions, and the connection represented what was essentially one-man rule. When some objected that this amounted to autocracy, Wesley's reply was that in joining up with him and his movement persons had voluntarily accepted his authority, and they were free to withdraw at any time they so chose. Following the death of Wesley the connection in Great Britain found center in the British Conference meeting annually. Methodism in the United States from 1792 on, found center in the General Conference. For the followers of Otterbein and Albright likewise it found center in the General Conference.

A Connectional Membership

The United Methodist Church has a connectional membership. Paragraph 109 of the *Discipline* states, "A member of any local United Methodist Church is a member of the total United Methodist connection." The connection as a whole sets the standards for membership in the particular local congregation, and the local church is not free to set membership standards of its own choosing. All members of all local churches are subject to the same *Discipline* of the one United Methodist Church and committed to the same vows. Members may transfer from one local United Methodist Church to another by the simple adjustment of local church records.

A Connectional Ministry

A still more obvious mark of United Methodism is the fact that it has a connectional ministry. That is to say that it has what is essentially one total ministerial force available for deployment to serve the total needs of the total church.

The early term used to describe this total ministry was "the traveling connection," and the term still appears at least in conference language. A ministerial candidate is received on trial, not just into an Annual Conference, but into the traveling connection. The use of such traditional conference language is but to affirm once again that a United Methodist minister, while being received on trial by an Annual Conference and having ministerial membership and voting privileges lodged in a particular Annual Conference, is in fact a part of the total ministry of the total church. In The United Methodist Church each minister is one unit in a total ministerial force of more than thirty-five thousand men and women, active and retired, who are committed to following the marching orders of the church and giving themselves as best they can to the total mission of the total church until finally God calls them from labor to rest. It is this total ministry for a total church which has again and again proven a source of amazement to people of other denominations, that has accounted in large measure for whatever effectiveness United Methodism has been able to achieve. It accounts for the fact that there is no United Methodist Church, large or small, without a preacher and no United Methodist preacher in the effective ranks without a church.

The episcopacy or the general superintendency is a part of this total ministry of the total church. The bishops of the church do not represent a separate ecclesiastical order. Rather they are elders like all other ministers in full connection, but elders who have been elected to fill a particular office to which the church has assigned particular responsibilities. For this reason bishops are no longer ordained as once was the custom in Methodism in earlier years, but are simply consecrated. Bishops in the United

Brethren and Evangelical churches were never regarded as a separate order and were subject to quadrennial election. For this reason the ceremony of induction was a quite simple one.

Connectional Amenability

United Methodism, in addition to having a connectional membership and ministry, has chosen to practice connectional amenability. Those who become members agree to be subject to the *Discipline* of the church. If they forget their vows or neglect their responsibilities as Christians they are subject to reprimand, correction, even trial, and in extreme cases to expulsion from membership. In earlier years close scrutiny of the membership of the societies was rigidly practiced, and it was not at all unusual for members to be dropped or even expelled. In later years severe disciplinary measures have not been generally exercised, but it is still expected that United Methodist members shall adhere faithfully to the ideals, both personal and social, cherished by The United Methodist Church.

United Methodist ministers are likewise amenable not only for their manner of life, but also for their official administration—the bishops to their respective Jursdictional Conferences and the ministers to their respective Annual Conferences. One of the oldest questions among those asked in United Methodist conferences is, "Are all the preachers blameless in their life and official administration?" The character of each minister must be passed annually by the Annual Conference and that of each bishop quadrennially by the Jurisdictional Conference. The examination of the life and character of the ministers was for long years conducted in open conference and was gone into in great detail. In connection with this, the ministers gave their reports on their labors of the previous year. Today, with much larger conferences and crowded business sessions, recommendations on the passage of ministerial character and administration come to the floor of the Annual Conference by way of the district superintendents or the Board of the Ministry.

The intent of this concept of amenability so deeply ingrained in United Methodism is not to impose undue restrictions upon either members or ministers, but simply to attempt to assure the integrity of the church as an effective instrument under God.

Connectional Ownership

Another important characteristic of The United Methodist Church is connectional ownership of property. United Methodist Church buildings and parsonages do not belong to the local congregations, but to the denomination as a whole. All deeds to United Methodist Church property if properly drawn, contain what is known as the trust clause which provides that the church building is to be used, kept, and maintained as a place of divine worship of the United Methodist ministry and members of the United Methodist Church subject to the *Discipline*, usage, and ministerial appointments of said church. A similar provision is required in parsonage deeds. This connectional ownership of church property has been tested in civil courts numerous times and again and again has been confirmed as valid.

An interesting feature of this connectional ownership of property is to be found in the provision of the *Discipline* with reference to abandonment of church property. When a local church becomes so weak that it can no longer continue, it becomes the responsibility of the Annual

Conference within whose bounds it is located to declare such church discontinued and to make disposition of the property. This provision acts upon the connectional principle that all church property belongs to the connection. The Annual Conference must, under the *Discipline,* take some action that results in the using of the funds realized from the sale of such abandoned property for further capital investment in church property. Thus, theoretically and in practicality, in United Methodism an investment once made in church property is never lost. When an original investment in church property at a particular point proves no longer necessary or desirable, at the discretion of the Annual Conference it is simply transferred to another point and is thus conserved for accomplishing the purposes for which it was intended by the original donors.

A Connectional Law-Making Body

At the summit of its structure The United Methodist Church as a connection has a supreme law-making body for the entire church. This is the General Conference, meeting regularly every four years and in special or called sessions at shorter intervals as the situation may warrant. It is democratically constituted being made up of lay and clerical delegates elected by all the respective Annual Conferences. It actions are final for the entire connection, except as any one of them, upon proper appeal, may be judged unconstitutional by the Judicial Council, the supreme judicial body of the church.

Connectional Guidance for Worship

United Methodism also provides for its churches and people connectional guidance for worship. When the

Methodist Episcopal Church in the United States was organized in 1784 Wesley sent over, for the use of the American Methodists, what was called *The Sunday Service*. This was an abridgement by his hand of *The Book of Common Prayer* of the Church of England. *The Sunday Service* did not meet with popular favor, however, and was soon abandoned.

Very early in all three churches ultimately constituting The United Methodist Church, hymnals were developed as aids to worship. In due time they became official, and new editions appeared on the average of every thirty to forty years.

Nothing has contributed more to connectional guidance in worship than the ritual of the church. This has represented a steady development across the years, including at first orders for baptism, the celebration of the Lord's Supper, ordination, marriage, and burial of the dead, with other orders being added in due time. This ritual of the church is official, being approved by the General Conference, and is expected to be used by our ministers and churches. Changes are made in it periodically by General Conference action, usually upon recommendation of some study commission bringing to the General Conference a detailed report for its consideration.

In more recent years connectional guidance for worship has been afforded by *The Book of Worship,* which contains a wealth of material for the enrichment of corporate, family, and private worship.

United Methodism does not insist upon uniformity in worship. Rather it allows for diversity in its congregations and among its people. For this reason the worship guidance material which it now makes available provides numerous optional forms.

With all the variations in worship found in different

United Methodist congregations there is still sufficient similarity that any United Methodist in attendance in any United Methodist congregation would normally have little difficulty in feeling fully at home.

Connectional Emphases

United Methodists have also long been marked by certain connectional emphases. To lay stress upon them has been traditional in United Methodism. It is to be remembered that Methodism, the Evangelical Association, and the United Brethren all began as evangelistic movements and not as efforts to propagate some new theology or to establish another church. Their emphasis in each case was upon the fact that God's salvation was freely available for all, that the miracle of the new birth could take place in the life of any person who would respond in faith, that such a person could come to enjoy full Christian assurance, that the believer was called upon to seek for Christian perfection and to be marked by holiness of heart and life, and that the followers of Christ should labor with all diligence to help create a redeemed society and to bind up the wounds of humanity.

These emphases have found expression in different ways as the years have come and passed. At times some of them have been stressed to the exclusion of others, but by and large they have continued to be the emphases which United Methodists have regarded and continue to regard as having supreme importance.

The way that the connectionalism of the church has held together across a period of roughly two centuries in the United Brethren Church, the Evangelical Association, and The Methodist Church probably represents one of the marvels of ecclesiastical history. It is a story eminently worth reading, but which cannot be gone into adequately in a writing of this character. There have been bitter battles at times, severe clashes, and sometimes withdrawals of individual members and groups whom the connection could ill afford to lose. But again there have been other times of succeeding in maintaining the fellowship despite marked differences of opinion, times of reconciliation, and times of reunion. In the main the connectionalism of United Methodism has held strong and, despite the strains of the present hour, promises to continue on into the indefinite future.

III

The Concept of Law

United Methodists have been across the years, and continue to be, a people governed by law. This is by their own voluntary agreement so far as individual members are concerned, each of them having agreed at the time of uniting with the church to be subject to its discipline. It is also by voluntary agreement so far as the church itself as a body is concerned. In the earliest days of the Methodist revival eight or ten persons who were deeply convicted of sin, on their own volition, came to John Wesley and asked for his help and advice. Out of this came the birth of the first Methodist societies and the giving of what are known as the General Rules. These simple practical guidelines were the forerunner of what we now know as the total body of United Methodist law. Also by voluntary agreement, in 1784 when Methodism in the United States was formally organized as a separate ecclesiastical body, the first American Methodists chose deliberately to be a people governed by law. Quadrennially as they have assembled in General Conference they have modified or added to the law of the church, thus continuing to ratify their choice to be a people governed by law. A similar pattern existed in the former United Brethren Church and the Evangelical Association.

As a people voluntarily choosing to be governed by law in whose development lay and clergy alike share, United Methodists stand in striking contrast to congregational churches, where each local congregation is a law unto itself, and to Roman Catholicism wherein tradition plays so large a role and authority is strongly associated with church councils and lodged ultimately in the papacy.

Law Embodied in a Book

For United Methodists the law by which they choose to be governed is embodied in a single volume published quadrennially. It is the book that they have long called *The Discipline*. Particularly among earlier Methodists, Evangelicals, and United Brethren, the *Discipline* of their respective churches was faithfully distributed by the preachers and was to be found in almost all the homes of active members where it was cherished along with the Bible and the hymnbook. The first Methodist *Discipline* to be issued was printed in 1785 following the Christmas Conference which organized the church. It was a small volume, only thirty-five pages in length, and consisted primarily of eighty-one questions with the answers given in the conference.

The Evangelical Association provided for its first *Discipline* in 1809 and the United Brethren in 1815.

In later years the *Discipline* perhaps has not had quite so prominent a place in the average United Methodist home, but it nevertheless is still sold in multiplied thousands of copies, is deeply reverenced by those who love the church and would know it intimately, and is an indispensible tool particularly for all who have official responsibility at any level of the church's life. It remains the chart by which the ongoing life of the church is guided continually.

It may be further observed that United Methodists have chosen to be a people governed by a body of law which is now quite extensive. The *Discipline* has expanded greatly with the years until today it is a large volume of more than six hundred pages, each page now twice the size of the *Disciplines* of only a few quadrennia ago. In addition, much material coming out of the General Conference that until recently was embodied in the *Discipline* itself is now printed separately in *The Book of Worship* and *The Book of Resolutions,* each of which is of considerable size.

United Methodists for some reason have persisted in going into great detail in writing church law. At this point they are scarcely paralleled by any other great ecclesiastical body. It seems to be a favorite sport among United Methodists for everyone to attempt to get his particular pet ideas embodied into church law, thus making them obligatory for everyone else. Strange to say, this tendency is no less pronounced among liberals in the church than among conservatives. There are, however, those United Methodists who feel that we go into too great detail in writing church law and that something would be gained if general directions and warrants of power were given without superimposing a large amount of carefully spelled-out, legal directions. This attitude obtains, particularly with reference to the operation of local churches and Annual Conferences, the feeling that they should be given larger freedom to determine their own course of action. The 1972 General Conference took note of this sentiment and allowed some larger latitude at these two points than has been granted before.

A Changing Book of Law

While United Methodists have chosen to be governed by a law embodied in a book, they have at the same time insisted that this shall be a changing book. They have updated their *Discipline* every four years and shall probably continue to do so on into the indefinite future. Back of this practice is the recognition of the importance of change and adaptability in the ongoing life of the church. Each succeeding General Conference of all the former denominations now composing United Methodism made certain changes in the *Discipline* of that church. Sometimes these changes were minor and represented only tinkering with church machinery, but at other times they were major and gave definite new direction to the life of the church. A brief comparison of our *Discipline* today with the *Discipline* of any one of the former churches of only a dozen years ago dramatizes vividly the habitual readiness of The United Methodist Church to look afresh at its body of church law and to make such changes as the times, situation, and mission warrant.

United Methodism recognizes, however, that some parts of its church law quite properly ought to be more difficult to change than others and that change in these parts of the law merits a vote by the entire church rather than simply a majority vote by the General Conference. These are those parts of United Methodist law which it is judged represent the basic structure of the church. This part of the *Discipline* is known as The Constitution. It covers some fifty pages of legislative material set at the beginning of the *Discipline* and represents the heart of the church law. Any part of it can be changed, but it can be changed only by a two-thirds vote of the General Conference and a subsequent two-thirds vote of the membership of all the Annual Conferences—clerical and lay, present and voting.

Likewise the Articles of Religion and the Confession of Faith cannot be revoked or altered without a two-thirds vote of the General Conference and a subsequent three-fourths vote in all the Annual Conferences.

All other parts of the *Discipline* may be changed by any General Conference by simple majority vote.

A Law Written by the People

United Methodists are a people choosing to be governed by a law which, in the end, they themselves have written. Technically United Methodist law is written by the General Conference, but in the fullest and truest sense it is written by the people of United Methodism themselves. The General Conference is a delegated body. It is the people of the church who in the Charge Conferences elect the lay delegates to the Annual Conferences, and it is the Annual Conferences which in turn elect the delegates, clerical and lay, to the General Conference. Whatever delegates may constitute any particular General Conference, it is after all the people who send them there, and it is the people whom they represent. There is no way for anyone to be a voting member of a General Conference except by election. All elections of delegates are by majority vote, and usually without formal nomination. It is difficult to conceive of a more genuinely democratic method of selecting the membership of a law-making body than that represented by the selection of the membership of a United Methodist General Conference.

More important still, the law of the United Methodist Church is written by the people of United Methodism in that they have the right of petition to the General Conference. Any individual United Methodist or group of Methodists may petition the General Conference upon any subject, and thousands of them do. The General Conference of 1972, for instance, received over twenty thousand petitions on some several thousand subjects from individual United Methodists or United Methodist groups all over the world. Every petition thus received receives respectful attention. Its receipt must be acknowledged in the columns of the *Daily Christian Advocate,* and it must be referred to the proper legislative committee where it must be duly considered. Each legislative committee must report its recommendation concerning each petition received by it, recommending either concurrence or nonconcurrence, and the General Conference in turn must act upon the recommendation of the legislative committee as it sees fit. The secretary of the General Conference is charged with the responsibility of seeing that every petition receives due attention and that the General Conference record shows the disposition made of it.

By this right of petition every individual United Methodist is assured of being heard with reference to the law of the church. In effect this is a privilege beyond that of members of the General Conference, for under the rules of the General Conference, members of that body, so far as new proposals in which they are interested are concerned, can make from the floor only a motion of reference to a committee, which is in effect exactly what any individual United Methodist does when he or she sends in a petition.

THE CONCEPT OF LAW

Law Subject to Interpretation

Finally United Methodists have chosen to be a people governed by law subject to review by a supreme judicial body. This is the Judicial Council of the church. It is constituted of nine persons, four lay and five clerical, elected by the General Conference by majority vote from a list of nominations submitted by the Council of Bishops plus nominations made from the floor. All jurisdictions of the church must be represented in the nominations, but not necessarily in the final election of members. Election is for an eight-year term. A panel of alternates is also provided for by election by the General Conference. Members of the Judicial Council cannot be members of the General Conference or of any United Methodist agency.

The Judicial Council is the final interpreter of United Methodist law. It has the power to determine the constitutionality of acts of the General Conference, to determine the legality of acts of various bodies such as a General, Jurisdictional, or Central Conference or a general agency, to hear appeals for declaratory decisions upon the part of certain designated bodies of the church, and under prescribed procedures to review the legal decisions made by the bishops in presiding over the conferences and either to confirm or reverse them. This power of review does not apply to parliamentary decisions made by the bishop. The appeal in this case is to the body. All decisions made by the Judicial Council are binding for the church.

The Judicial Council meets regularly twice a year to review matters properly before it. Its decisions are published following each meeting in pamphlet form and quadrennially in a bound volume. Decisions of the Judicial Council to date total some three hundred sixty, and they represent a careful and enlightening and stimulating commentary upon United Methodist law.

For long years in the former churches now represented by The United Methodist Church there was considerable discussion as to where the final responsibility for the interpretation of church law should be lodged. In some cases it was with the bishops as a collegiate body and in some cases with the General Conference itself in effect making it the interpreter of its own actions. Finally in the Methodist Episcopal Church, South, a Judicial Council was established in 1934. This polity feature was carried over into The Methodist Church in 1939 and in turn into The United Methodist Church in 1968.

Finally it may be observed that United Methodist law is enforced by United Methodists themselves by way of voluntary compliance. The bishops are charged to uphold the law in the respective conferences, the district superintendents in the districts, and the pastors in the churches. But in the end the keeping of the law of the church is today largely a matter of acceptance upon the part of all concerned. There are now few church trials and still fewer expulsions, and resort to the civil courts is seldom taken. A few mavericks occasionally disregard or flout the law of the church, but all in all United Methodists accept its guidance and choose to abide by it. They think of themselves as a people in covenant who have voluntarily made themselves a people governed by law.

IV

The Concept of the Church

The United Methodist Church in its Articles of Religion defines the visible church of Christ as "a congregation of faithful men in which the pure Word of God is preached, and the Sacraments duly administered according to Christ's ordinance, in all things that of necessity are requisite to the same" (Article XIII).

The Confession of Faith, taken over from the Evangelical United Brethren Church is fuller, of more recent composition, and couched in what is more the language of the present day. It defines the church as "the community of all true believers under the Lordship of Christ." It affirms that it is "one, holy, apostolic and catholic." It further defines it as "the redemptive fellowship in which the Word of God is preached by men divinely called, and the sacraments are duly administered according to Christ's own appointment." It goes on to declare that "the Church exists for the maintenance of worship, the edification of believers and the redemption of the world" (Article V).

United Methodism therefore thinks of the church pri-

29

marily as people related to Christ—the people composing it and the people ministering in and through it. It does not think first of the church in terms of organization, although it has been largely given to organization and has been accused by its critics of being overorganized. Neither does it think first of the church in terms of buildings, although particularly in later years it has gone in strongly for church buildings most of which stand in striking contrast to the simplicity of Methodist, Evangelical, and United Brethren chapels of an earlier day, a simplicity which incidentally our fathers in the faith insisted upon, not for economic reasons, but as a matter of conscience and conviction.

Committed People

United Methodism thinks of the church as being made up of committed people. In the words of the Articles it speaks of them as "faithful men" and in the words of the Confession as "true believers." It does not think of the church as being made up of perfect persons, but it does think of it as being made up of persons who believe, who take religion seriously, who trust Christ completely, and who sincerely want to "go on to perfection."

People in Association for Worship and Service

United Methodism thinks of the church as being made up of committed people in association. Its emphasis at this point has always been a strong one. The words used in the Articles are "the congregation of faithful men," and the words used in the Confession are "the community of all true believers" and "the redemptive fellowship." It is in and through association that members of the church find mutual support, experience spiritual growth, and find ways and means of meeting their full Christian responsibilities.

United Methodists think of the church as a worshiping community. The Articles stress the preaching of "the pure Word of God," and the Confession of Faith moves a step further and adds "preached by men divinely called." Both the Articles and the Confession lift up the importance of the sacraments and insist that they be "duly administered" even as Christ commanded.

In addition to thinking of the church as a worshiping community The United Methodist Church thinks of it also as a serving community. There is no mention of this idea in the Articles of Faith regarding the church, which Wesley took over long ago from the Articles of the Church of England. But it has been traditional among Methodists from the beginning to insist that the church move beyond its doors to seek the lost and bring them to Christ, to establish institutions ministering to human needs of all types, and to reform society. So strong has been this insistence that the so-called activism of the Methodists was once often scorned in some religious circles. The United Brethren and Evangelical churches followed the same pattern and witnessed their phenomenal early growth largely as a result of their unwearying and effective evangelistic activity.

In recent years there has been throughout the Christian world a new strong insistence upon the church's moving beyond its doors. For those in the United Methodism tradition this insistence has served but to call them back to their first love and their original pattern of operation. The Confession of Faith puts this idea into strong words as it affirms that the church exists not only for the maintenance of worship and the edification of believers, but also "for the redemption of the world."

An Inclusive Fellowship

United Methodism insists that this fellowship of the church for worship and service shall be an inclusive fellowship. It thinks of the church as the proper place where the rich and poor meet together and God is the Father of them all. It believes that the church should know no barriers represented by race, culture, or economic status. Not all United Methodist churches are the inclusive congregations cutting across economic, cultural, and racial lines that they should be and in many cases would perhaps even like to be. Sometimes this is due to the accident of location in a neighborhood made up of only one type of resident. Sometimes it is due to the feeling of some persons that they would not be truly welcome. Again it is due to a simple slowness upon the part of some people of different races or culture to break with older patterns that have long been familiar to them. Sometimes it is due to no more than the failure to make the effort which inclusiveness involves, to inability to understand just how to go about achieving true inclusiveness.

The story of the progress that has been made toward achieving genuine inclusiveness in United Methodism, particularly across racial lines, is a long and challenging one. It has its sad chapters and sometimes the rate of progress has been all too slow, but nevertheless the movement has generally been in a forward direction.

From the beginning the Methodist Episcopal Church in the United States had black members. After the division of Methodism in 1844 the Methodist Episcopal Church, South, likewise had black members of local congregations until 1870 when they formed the independent Colored Methodist Episcopal Church, now called the

Christian Methodist Episcopal Church. The local churches of the Methodist Protestant Church were likewise open to blacks. The Evangelical United Brethren churches, having been over so many years made up primarily of German-speaking immigrants and their descendants, had almost no black membership at the time of union in 1968.

With the close of the Civil War the Methodist Episcopal Church began to move into the South to establish greatly needed school for blacks. It also began to form Annual Conferences. At first these were fully integrated conferences. Shortly, a movement developed to establish separate Annual Conferences for blacks. The argument often made was that the black congregations would stand to gain this way. Strong resistance was offered particularly by Bishop Gilbert Haven who felt that any separation in church structure based upon race was a denial of the church's essential nature. Nevertheless, with the encouragement of much of both the white and black leadership of the church, such racial conferences were established. They wrote a notable record, and there were nineteen of them at the time of Methodist union in 1939.

With Methodist union in 1939 the Negro Annual Conferences were set up as a Central Jurisdiction with all the rights and privileges of every other jurisdiction. Whatever else may be said for or against the Central Jurisdiction —and many black Methodists were never happy about it —it did represent a strong power base for assured black representation in the total life of the church. The Central Jurisdiction passed out of existence in 1968.

At length the time came when the church arrived at the conclusion that any form of racial exclusiveness was wrong, and the *Discipline* now provides that no unit of the church shall be structured so as to exclude anyone upon the basis of race. In late days serious effort is being made to move in the direction of a fully open itinerancy serving the churches regardless of their racial composition. All in all, the new adjustments in the life of the church ignoring racial lines are working quite well.

However far from the ideal the situation may be in some of its local churches, United Methodism as a church officially takes the position that each of its congregations must be open to all people and affirms that a local church should be truly representative of humanity itself. The *Discipline* provides that "all persons without regard to race, color, natural origin or economic condition shall be eligible to attend its worship services, to participate in its programs, and when they take the appropriate vows to be admitted into its membership in any local church in the connection."

Other Churches

The same description of a church which United Methodism accepts for itself, it applies in its thinking to other denominations. It regards them as churches if they represent fellowships that seek to be redemptive wherein the gospel is preached and the sacraments are duly administered. It unchurches no other church. It does not judge them by their theology or their form of government or the rituals which they practice, but rather by their commitment to Christ and his kingdom. Because United Methodism does not unchurch other evangelical churches, it receives church members from and transfers members to other churches without other formality except the simple issuance or receipt of a church letter.

In recognizing other evangelical churches as truly churches, United Methodism in turn is forced to think of itself as "a church" rather than as "the church." By taking this rather broad position United Methodism doubtlessly loses its appeal to some people who are anxious to belong to "the church" rather than simply to "a church" and who welcome a strong authoritarian church claim. Nevertheless United Methodism like its predecessors does not feel that it can take, nor does it desire to take, anything less than a broad church position.

This is not to overlook the fact that there have been periods when some of our forebears did take strong exception to other denominations and sometimes did battle with them. A hundred years ago church debates were popular, and there were those argumentative preachers in the United Methodist tradition who entered into these, with vigor and enthusiasm and skill and those lay persons who attended them with avid interest and relish. During this period it was popular to publish pamphlets on such subjects as "Why I am not a Baptist," "Why I am not an Episcopalian," or a member of some other communion. Despite this chapter in its history the general position of the United Methodist tradition has been that all other evangelical churches were to be acknowledged and respected as true churches of Jesus Christ and that the battle is to be against sin in all its varied personal and social forms rather than against others of the household of faith.

The last fifty years have witnessed not only as previously the acknowledgement of other churches upon the part of United Methodism, but, what is more important, the development of cordial working relationships with them through the National Council of Churches, the World Council of Churches, and the Methodist World Council.

A development in recent years of particular interest has been in the field of relationships with the Roman Catholic Church from which for long years, like other Protestants, Methodists were widely separated, the separation upon the part of both bodies at times reaching the point of bitter antagonism. The 1970 General Conference adopted a resolution reinterpreting, by setting in historical perspective, those portions of the Articles of Religion relative to the Roman Church and its practices which in rather strong language reflect the sometimes bitter feeling that attended on occasion the struggle to establish the Protestant Reformation.

Another development in recent years in the field of relationships with other churches has been United Methodism's participation in the Consultation on Church Union.

United Methodists whenever they repeat the Apostles' Creed affirm once again their faith and thinking regarding the church, in the simple, eloquent, and significant words, "I believe in . . . the holy catholic Church." It is not only The United Methodist Church in which they believe, but the universal church of Christ existing across the ages and scattered throughout the earth and constituted not only of all those souls everywhere who live by faith in the Son of God, but likewise of those who have died in the faith, but who are yet forever a part of the church.

This holy, catholic church, United Methodists strongly believe, under God "will be preserved to the end of time for the conduct of worship, the due administration of his word and sacraments, the maintenance of Christian fellowship and discipline, the edification of believers and the conversion of the world."

V

The Concept of Membership

Every United Methodist congregation represents a company of people who have voluntarily associated themselves together with a specific spiritual purpose in mind. And all United Methodist congregations whether they be large or small, rural or urban, having large resources or having few resources, in theory at least, are committed to the same spiritual purpose.

Each local church, according to the definition of the *Discipline,* is a "connectional society of persons who have professed their faith in Christ, have been baptized, have assumed the vows of membership . . . and are associated in fellowship . . . 'in order that they may hear the word of God, receive the Sacraments, and carry forward the work which Christ has committed to his Church'" (Paragraph 103).

Membership in The United Methodist Church is open to any and all persons willing to take the vows of membership.

UNITED METHODISM IN THEORY AND PRACTICE

A People of Faith

United Methodist members are expected first of all to be a people of faith. The primary question asked of those being baptized is, "Do you truly and earnestly repent of your sins and accept Jesus Christ as your Savior?" And the primary question asked upon admission into church membership is, "Do you confess Jesus Christ as your Lord and Savior and pledge your allegiance to his kingdom?" The assumption of these questions is that those admitted to membership have exercised faith to receive forgiveness for past sins and to experience the renewal of their hearts that they now look to Christ for the supplying of all their spiritual needs, and that they see in him the one and only Lord of life and are resolved to do and to be what his lordship demands.

The United Methodist Church is not a creedal church in the sense that all United Methodists are expected to subscribe unhesitatingly to a closely detailed system of doctrine. There is nowhere in United Methodism a detailed system as is officially set forth in the confessions of some other churches, and there are no particular theological textbooks that are officially designated as standard for the denomination. This does not mean, however, that United Methodism is not committed to basic Christian doctrine. The Articles of Religion have been a part of every Methodist *Discipline* since the church was established in 1784. They came to Methodism in the United States by way of Wesley and represented his abridgement of the Thirty-nine Articles of the Church of England. They represent basic beliefs which many Christians of every denomination share in common, and they identify United Methodists with the broad sweep of Protestant tradition.

THE CONCEPT OF MEMBERSHIP

The Evangelical Association in 1809 upon the recommendation of George Miller adopted a German translation of the Methodist Articles of Religion and added an article of their own on "The Last Judgment." These Articles were further reduced and consolidated to become in 1839 constitionally unchangeable.

The United Brethren Church beginning in 1813 developed what was known as the Confession of Faith which was declared unalterable in 1841. A new Confession was approved, however, in 1889, but resulted in a division of the church.

The Evangelical United Brethren did adopt a new Confession of Faith in 1962, and this was brought over into union in 1968.

Both the Articles of Religion and the Confession of Faith are embodied in the *Discipline* as the doctrinal standards of the church. In addition it is specified that Wesley's *Sermons* and his *Notes on the New Testament* are included in the existing and established standards of doctrine.

The General Conference of 1972 declared that all these are to be accepted as landmark documents for United Methodists. They represent a great treasury of truth and are part of a rich heritage from the past.

In addition to these spelled-out doctrinal statements, United Methodism is the inheritor of those common emphases that have marked from the beginning all the churches represented in United Methodist union. These include emphases upon the grace of God freely available for all; upon salvation by faith alone, upon the experience of conversion and new life in Christ, upon Christian assurance, upon holiness of heart and life, and upon going on to perfection. These emphases have been lifted up repeatedly in United Methodist preaching and teaching and testimony, and they find particular embodiment in the Wesleyan hymns.

United Methodists are challenged by their church to do serious theological thinking especially in a day like the present, to be fully open to new light, to be appreciative of the theological insights of others, and to test all theological concepts in the light of Scripture, tradition, experience, and reason.

Committed to Fellowship

Just as United Methodist members are expected to be a people of faith, so also are they expected to be a people committed to fellowship. No one of the great denominations has laid greater stress upon the importance of fellowship than has United Methodism. In fact the original groups first known as Methodists were nothing more than religious fellowships. These were not churches, and in the beginning it was never dreamed that they would evolve in time into churches. They were merely religious societies made up primarily of members of the Church of England. John Wesley never desired them to be anything else, and the very term he chose to denominate them, "the United Societies," spoke volumes at this point. They were simply groups of people "desiring to flee from the wrath to come and to be saved from their sins," to use the now quaint language of that day. Wesley himself defined such fellowships as "a company of men having the form and seeking the power of godliness united in order to pray together, to receive the work of exhortation, and to watch over one another in love that they may help each other to work out their salvation." To make the fellowship of the societies still more effective each society was divided into classes and bands thus providing for the more intimate fellowship of a still smaller group.

The stress of the United Brethren upon the importance of Christian fellowship is forcefully dramatized in the very name that they chose for themselves as a church. The similar stress in the Evangelical Association is also reflected in the name which they chose for themselves.

While changes have occurred as the years have passed in the way that such fellowship finds expression among them, United Methodists continue to be a people stressing the high importance of Christian fellowship. They know that faith is born in fellowship, that it grows in fellowship, and that it finds its fullest expression in and through fellowship. Hence comes the strong United Methodist emphasis upon the importance of congregational worship, upon the value of group association for prayer and study and action, and upon the necessity for total congregational involvement in multiplied forms of glad and sacrificial Christian activity.

Committed to Growth

United Methodists members are also expected to be people committed to Christian growth. United Methodists have always strongly stressed not only the necessity for persons to be Christians, but in addition the necessity of their becoming better Christians. The early Evangelicals and United Brethren and Methodists all talked much about sanctification and perfect love and the fully surrendered life and about "going on to perfection." Much of this earlier language has become less common with United Methodists of a later day, but the basic idea thus stressed by the fathers is still accepted and held to be a valid objective. United Methodism still insists that its people shall be constantly growing spiritually.

The Christian growth thus contemplated necessarily involves commitment to worship. There is no real spiritual growth apart from worship. Hence United Methodism stresses today as it has always done the importance of public worship and asks all its members to support the church by their presence. Recently there has been increasing attention given to making the worship experience more meaningful for the congregation, and later years have witnessed the coming into being of a rich supply of new worship aids. Similarly there is no real spiritual growth apart from private worship. It has been well observed that "no man is truly properly religious until he is devout." Hence United Methodism has always urged and continues to urge its members to give themselves with all diligence to private prayer, meditation, and regular reading of the Scriptures.

Family worship likewise contributes to Christian growth. United Methodists have always known this, and at one time the family altar was the obvious mark of a typical Methodist, Evangelical, or United Brethren home. With the passing of the day when life centered largely in the home, particularly the farm home and the small town home as it once did, family worship began to decline. When the Methodist Episcopal Church, South, in 1934 gave to the world *The Upper Room,* it stimulated a revival of family worship the force of which is still growing as this family devotional periodical carries forward its quiet but tremendously effective ministry through some three million copies published bimonthly in some forty languages and forty-seven editions and distributed throughout the world.

THE CONCEPT OF MEMBERSHIP

Commitment to Discipline

The Christian growth expected of United Methodists involves likewise commitment to discipline. There can be no genuine Christian growth apart from discipline. The early Methodists knew this, and at their own request they received from Wesley a listing of certain standards of conduct known as the General Rules. These were a part of every Methodist *Discipline* from the beginning. Even as late as forty years ago it was required that each preacher read them annually to every congregation, and he was under obligation to report to the Quarterly Conference whether or not he had done so. The specifics of these rules written by Wesley reflect the common temptations, sins, and foibles of the day in which they were written, as Wesley and the early Methodists saw them, some of which are still the undoing of countless individuals and of society. One would probably not embody all the same specifics were a set of guidelines being written for disciplined living today, but the three overall imperatives which the General Rules lift up still hold, namely (1) doing no harm by avoiding evil of every kind, (2) doing good; by being in every kind, merciful after their power; as they have opportunity, doing good of every possible sort, and, as far as possible to all men, and (3) attending upon the ordinances of God.

While after the General Rules were given by Wesley, no additional formalized statement of personal disciplines to be observed was developed in Methodism, and while the Evangelical and United Brethren churches did not see fit to develop comparable statements, nevertheless in all three churches similar traditions with reference to proper conduct for churches members developed which were so pronounced as to have strong binding effect. Thinking has changed some among United Methodists particularly at the point of some things once termed "worldly," but it is still expected that United Methodists shall be a people committed to purity of life, sobriety, self-control, and the highest standards of personal conduct.

Beginning early in the present century it came to be realized that Christian people needed not only guidance for personal living, but that they and society at large needed guidance for social living as well.

Hence there was developed in the Methodist Episcopal Church, under the guidance of persons such as Bishops Welch and McConnell, Dr. Frank Mason North, and others, what came to be known as the Social Creed. This was adopted by the General Conference of 1908. Later in the same year the Social Creed was approved by the Federal Council of Churches.

The Methodist Episcopal Church, South, adopted a Social Creed in 1914. The Methodist Protestant Church, the Evangelical Association, and the United Brethren Church all adopted similar creeds in the same general era. The Evangelical United Brethren Church adopted a Statement of Social Principles in 1946.

The 1972 General Conference approved a new Statement of Social Principles, embodying many things mentioned in former statements, but also adding many other things unmentioned heretofore. The decision of the 1968 General Conference calling for a new statement grew out of a recognition of the totally new social situation in which the church now finds itself.

The statement was developed by a commission representing persons from all areas of the church's life, who devoted long hours to its preparation. It deals with many facets of the social situation and goes into great detail.

The territory covered is so great that it is scarcely to be expected that every United Methodist would find himself or herself in full agreement with the statement at every particular point.

The statement was submitted to the General Conference of 1972, and there it was amended at several points after lengthy floor debate. In a few cases the vote count on amendments was quite close. The statement as finally adopted represents therefore the majority opinion of the General Conference delegates present and voting. It can be changed by the same process in any future General Conference. As thus adopted it does represent the official position of The United Methodist Church on the issues touched upon, for by definition only the General Conference can speak officially for the church.

The statement is sent down to the people of the church for their guidance as they face the mounting complexities of society today. Ultimately it stands or falls with them, according to the logic of its argument and the persuasiveness of the case which it seeks to make.

Committed to Action

It is to be added that United Methodist members are expected to be persons committed to action. They are asked to be witnesses to their faith in every area of their lives. They are asked to take Christian positions and to stand by them, even though such stand may prove costly. They are asked to be evangelists and to be concerned about any and all who are without Christ and to seek to bring them to a knowledge of him. They are asked to engage in such Christian action of any and all forms as promises to bring into being a better world. They are

45

asked to give of their time, resources, energies, and love of their hearts in a fully committed stewardship to the end that the kingdom of God may come among men. In the words of the *Discipline* every member of The United Methodist Church "is to be a servant of Christ on mission in the local and worldwide community" (Paragraph 113).

The Children of the Church

Finally United Methodist members are expected to dedicate their children to Christ in baptism, to live before them an exemplary Christian life, to train them in the Christian faith, and thus to pave the way for them when they have reached the age of discretion, to take the vows of membership for themselves. The baptized children of United Methodist Church members constitute the prepatory roll of each local church. This roll is to be kept in each church with great care. Names are added to it as children are baptized and taken from it as their families remove from the local church or as such children having reached the proper age become full members of the church. Each pastor is under obligation to arrange regularly for classes for training in church membership for children who preferably have completed the sixth grade. Following training in such confirmation classes the children enrolled are received into full membership.

Training in the meaning of church membership is also called for by the *Discipline* for those who have delayed until adult years seeking admission into the church.

For long years in earlier Methodism, candidates for membership were received at first only on probation and were admitted into full membership only after they had given evidence of the sincerity of their faith and purpose.

The rigid probationary period was dropped about a century ago.

It is expected that the taking of membership vows shall be in the presence of the congregation except when some valid reason makes this impossible.

A Life Commitment

For United Methodists taking the vows of church membership represents a life commitment. It is to be expected, of course, that some who take United Methodist vows will, for reasons adequate to them, see fit later to transfer to other Christian fellowships, and provision is made for such transfer. It must also be acknowledged, to be realistic, that all too many who take the membership vows in time fall away or even deliberately turn their backs upon their decision, and again provision is made in the law for first seeking to reclaim these for Christ and the church, or if this proves impossible, to accept with sorrow their decision and remove their names from the roll.

But what is expected and hoped for is that those taking the membership vows will keep their commitment to Christ and to his church unto the end. So strong was this hope in an earlier day in Methodism that Methodist roll books once contained a column marked "Manner of Death," and early Methodist preachers entered carefully in the church record some notation regarding the final triumph of members finishing their course. Likewise in an earlier day the congregation in receiving members expressed this expectation and hopes through the words of the preacher, as he said in the name of the church, to those being received, "We pray that you may be numbered with his people here and with his saints in glory everlasting." The language of the ritual for receiving members into the church has of course changed some with the years, but United Methodism still believes as it always has that commitment to Christ and his church should be a commitment not only *of* all of life, but also *for* all of life.

VI

The Concept of the Ordained Ministry

In at least one important respect the United Methodist concept of the ministry differs radically from that of any other Protestant church. This needs to be understood clearly by United Methodists themselves in the course of the regular ongoing life of the church and by our brethren of other denominations when, along with them, we may be considering together possibilities for union. Parenthetically it should be observed that The United Methodist Church does not claim for its ministry a validity which it denies to the ministry of other churches. Our great concern with reference to any ministry for a united church is not at this point.

A Team Ministry

The peculiar feature of the Methodist concept of the ministry is that first of all it is designed to be a team ministry. It is a team ministry created by and for the connection as a whole. The Annual Conference becomes for the

49

United Methodist minister the door into the traveling connection and represents the particular unit of the connection to which he or she is accountable and serves, but essentially all United Methodist ministers are a part of the total ministry of the total church. This ministry created by the connection is created for the purpose of supplying all the local churches and all the other ministerial needs of the connection.

A Ministry Bound by Commitments

The United Methodist ministry is a team ministry bound by the same commitments. Every United Methodist minister must answer the same questions before admission into full connection and take the same ordination vows. These obligations have much in common with the obligations assumed by the ministers of other churches, but they include one additional commitment and that is the commitment to a team ministry represented by the agreement to take one's marching orders from the conference. For long years now consultation of one form or another with both ministers and churches regarding possible pastoral appointments has been practiced, but the final decision in every appointment still remains with the connection.

A Mobile Ministry

The United Methodist ministry is a team ministry designed to be mobile. This is the basic connotation of the long-used term "itinerant." This term is applied across the board to the ministry, including the episcopacy. For long years United Methodism's favorite designation for its ministry was "the itinerancy." This mobile ministry was designed originally for various purposes—to make it possible to follow the frontier, to shepherd the scattered and often weak congregations, and at one time even to care for the problem of a ministry not sufficiently trained to serve effectively too long in any one place. Across the years United Methodism has been able to keep its ministry as a whole fairly fluid and thus to adjust readily to changing situations as they have arisen.

The United Methodist ministry is a team ministry deployed periodically to meet the total needs of the total church. Here is where the Annual Conference session and the responsibility of the bishop for making appointments come to the fore. The coming of the Annual Conference session, with the final item on its agenda being the stationing of the preachers for another year, affords a regularly recurring opportunity to face at the same time situations in the respective local churches which need adjustment and work them out together as a part of a total picture. Every set of annual appointments should mean, and can mean, the careful deployment of a total team with each minister being given opportunity to play the best possible role and make a particular contribution toward the achievement of total team effectiveness.

The United Methodist concept of a team ministry, in the light of the above, goes therefore beyond that of a ministry merely bound together by a certain team spirit. It rather envisages a ministry in which the individual minister chooses to merge with the larger group that the total needs of the total church may be met by way of a total team.

An Interwoven Character

The team ministry of United Methodism tends to take on an interwoven character that can scarcely be matched elsewhere. The lives of the ministers of a particular Annual Conference become more and more interrelated as the years come and go, and the feeling grows increasingly among them that what happens to one affects all. Annual Conference journals carry a role of the honored dead thus suggesting that all ministers who have ever been a part of the Annual Conference in a sense continue so to be, even though they have joined the church triumphant. At least one Annual Conference, the Holston, has a conference cemetery high on the hill overlooking the Emory and Henry campus in southwest Virginia. It has been there for well over a hundred years, and there many of Holston's sons and daughters have found their final resting place. It symbolizes the intimacy of a team ministry and seems to keep saying silently but dramatically, "We were one in life and we are one forever."

A Called Ministry

In order that it may have such a team ministry, United Methodism asks that its ministers be persons conscious of a divine call to which they respond with glad commitment. It asks of those whom it ordains, "Do you trust that you are inwardly moved by the Holy Spirit to take upon you the office of the ministry in the Church of Christ?" It recognizes that this call of God may and does come to different persons in different ways, but it holds that only the sustaining encouragement of a sense of call can finally make one sufficient for the exactions particularly of a team ministry. It realizes also that this sense of call can become dull with the passing of the years to the hurt of the minister's effectiveness and that it can even be lost. It therefore makes possible honorable location or permits withdrawal for that minister who reaches the point where in the words of our fathers he wishes to "cease to travel."

An Expendable Ministry

As a team ministry, the United Methodist ministry is expected to be an expendable one, and this in fact it indeed is. Every United Methodist minister promises to go where sent, and though sometimes not going too happily, the average minister still faithfully adheres to the ordination vows. The United Methodist minister being thus expendable has no assurance of salary beyond the minimum set by the conference and no claim for unpaid salary should the appointed charge prove unable to meet its financial obligations in any particular year. While those who constitute the United Methodist ministry today may feel the need to confess that they are actually not as expendable as they might be, the record of the past for the United Methodist ministry as a whole is by and large one of splendid and shining devotion. At one time it was even common practice for the bishops of the Evangelical Association and the United Brethren Church to pause in the midst of the business of the Annual Conference and ask the members of the conference who were willing to go even to the hardest appointments if necessary to meet the needs of the church to stand silently to their feet, and a dramatic response was never lacking.

A Shared Support

As a team and as an expendable ministry, the United Methodist ministry is designed to be one that shares and shares alike so far as ministerial support is concerned. All ministerial support items are based upon the salary received by the pastor. The funds for the support of the episcopacy and the district superintendency and funds for pensions and minimum salaries are all related on a ratio basis to the pastor's salary. If the salary of the pastor is paid in full, these too must be paid in full; and if it is not paid in full these funds are to be shorted proportionally. Back of this provision lies the assumption that all the ministry of United Methodism is one ministry forever intimately related.

United Methodism accepts full responsibility for the support of this committed team ministry through which it seeks to accomplish its work. It guarantees an appointment to every minister until the age of seventy-two years so long as the person's character and administration are acceptable. It does not guarantee a necessarily desirable appointment or one of his or her particular choosing, but it does guarantee a place to serve.

Normally it supplies a parsonage for the minister's family. The purpose of a parsonage is not to supplement the income of the minister, although in practical effect it does this. Rather the basic purpose of having parsonages is to continue to make possible the mobility of the church's ministry and to avoid the necessity of facing annually the question of possible places of residence for the freshly deployed ministerial force of the conference.

Today every United Methodist minister is guaranteed by the conference a minimum salary, no matter what may be the financial strength of the charge the minister is appointed to serve. The minimum salary scale is set by each Annual Conference as it may determine. Certain variants in the figure finally set are allowed, such as number of dependents or years of service, according to the choice of the Annual Conference.

The new term for what was formerly known as minimum salary is "equitable salary." Back of this provision of the *Discipline* is the assumption that some salary floor is only logical in the case of a genuinely team ministry.

Furthermore The United Methodist Church supports its ministry by providing pensions for ministers who have reached retirement age and for the widows and dependents of deceased ministers. Pension rates are fixed by each Annual Conference, and payments to pensioners are made upon the basis of years of service. In earlier years pension funds were frequently distributed upon the basis of the necessity of each claimant, but this proved difficult to establish, and finally the church moved in the direction of the present, actually more just, basis of the same pension for every pensioner of the conference for the same number of years of service.

A Trained Ministry

United Methodism insists that its team ministry shall be a trained ministry. John Wesley himself set the pattern for this in his careful plans for the training of his lay preachers through providing books for them to read, guiding their studies, and making possible for them study centers such as the New Room at Bristol.

In pioneer days, the Methodists, the Evangelicals, and the United Brethren provided a form of training of young ministers by appointing them as junior preachers serving under and with an experienced preacher. Thus they learned, in the school of experience, the work of the ministry by doing it.

In due time courses of study covering the first four years of ministerial service became required. At first these courses of study were selected by the bishops of the church, and the whole training program thus established was designed and carried through by them. Later with the establishment of general church educational agencies, the responsibility for the course of study program was lodged with them. There it remained for long years, much of the work being taken by the ministers by correspondence.

The Methodists, United Brethren, and Evangelicals were all slow at first to develop seminaries as there were those even in the episcopacy of the church who feared that too much learning might undermine piety and zeal. About the middle of the nineteenth century, however, all three churches did begin to develop seminaries, and today every United Methodist preacher is expected to have seminary training, and the church has developed generous support plans for both student and institutions to make this possible.

Today, United Methodism also realizes that an adequately trained ministry must be a ministry that continues to be trained, and hence it lays strong emphasis upon the continuing education of ministers including even those who have spent long years in the active ministry.

Entrance into the Ministry

Entrance into the ministry of The United Methodist Church is by way of the Annual Conference after proper training and upon recommendation of the Conference Board of the Ministry and by vote of the conference. Admission is at first into probationary membership which is a trial period of two years during which the candidate has opportunity to decide whether to continue as a United Methodist minister, and the conference has opportunity to test out the gifts, grace, and possible degree of usefulness of this candidate. At the conclusion of the probationary period, the candidate is, by vote of the conference, received into full conference membership following satisfactory answers to the questions for admission into full connection. These questions were prepared originally by John Wesley and have been asked of every Methodist minister prior to 1968 and are now asked of each new United Methodist minister.

Upon election by the conference the ministerial candidate is eligible for deacon's orders at the time of admission on trial and for elder's orders at the time of admission into full connection. Ordination is by one of the bishops of the church.

Ministers who cannot meet the full requirements for conference membership may be received as associate members after meeting certain specifications for associate membership. Associate members are under the same obligation to go where they are sent as are full members of the conference.

Women in the Ministry

For long years the ministry of the Methodist churches and the Evangelical and United Brethren churches was open only to men. At first the fact that only men were admitted into the ministry seems to have been simply the result of practice. The legislation with reference to the ministry did make repeated use of the masculine pronoun only. In due time, therefore, as clergy rights for women became a live issue, there were legal decisions by conservative and strict constructionist interpreters of the law that the legislation of the church did not admit women to the church's ministry. These decisions appear to have been based largely upon the exclusive use of the male pronoun in the legislation rather than upon any spelled-out prohibition against admitting women as ministers. As decisions, they seem to reflect the male mind of an earlier age in the history of the church and of the world.

The battle for clergy rights for women was a long and difficult one. At first certain halfway steps were taken such as providing that women could become lay preachers. At length in 1956 the battle was won in The Methodist Church by the adoption by the General Conference of a single sentence of legislation affirming that "women are included in the provisions of all the foregoing legislation." Today many women are members of Annual Conferences, and as such they are fully eligible under the law for appointment to a pastorate, a district superintendency, a special appointment, or for election to the episcopacy.

Special Appointments

For long years in the earlier days all United Methodist ministers were appointed either to the pastorate of a charge, to a district superintendency, or to a connectional office of the Annual Conference or the general church. There was no provision for appointment to what later came to be called "special appointments," and those interested in certain types of specialized ministry were forced to locate as in the case of the famous William Taylor who was forced to locate in order to give himself to full-time evangelism and missionary work of his own enterprising, but was later elected a bishop. Gradually the law has been changed across the years to allow for appointment of conference members to numerous and diverse ministries of various kinds, some of them only loosely related to the church if at all. With today's rather broad concept of what ministry conceivably may and should involve, there are many United Methodist ministers who feel called to specialized ministries of many

58

and sundry kinds, many of them in the secular world. Such ministers are free to be appointed to these ministries and still retain their conference membership provided there is definite request for such appointment, the cabinet recommends, the Annual Conference approves by a two-thirds vote, and the bishop agrees to make the appointment.

A Dedicated Ministry

Every United Methodist minister is asked to make a complete dedication of himself to the highest ideals of the Christian life and to agree to exercise responsible self-control by personal habits conducive to bodily health, mental and emotional maturity, social responsibility, growth in grace, and the knowledge and love of God.

United Methodist ministers are bound in special covenant to perform their ministerial duties and to maintain the ministerial standards of the church. They offer themselves without reserve to be appointed and to serve as their superiors in office may direct. They live with their fellow ministers in mutual trust and concern and seek with them the sanctification of the fellowship (Paragraph 331).

VII

The Concept of the Episcopacy

The episcopacy in United Methodism is unlike that of any other church having episcopacy as a part of its structure. Another term for the episcopacy in United Methodism is "the general superintendency."

An Office

With United Methodists the episcopacy is an office and not an order. A bishop remains only an elder who has been set aside for a specific function. The fact that election to the episcopacy in United Methodism, except in certain Central Conferences, is for life, does not reflect the judgment that the episcopacy is something sacrosanct, but rather the conviction that men exercising the episcopal office in an appointive system such as United Methodism should be free from the inevitable pressures that might attend being subject to periodic reelection.

Furthermore, the episcopacy in United Methodism makes no claim to historic succession. The only request made by United Methodism of the remainder of the Christian world regarding its episcopacy is that both it and the United Methodist ministry be judged by their fruits.

Again, the episcopacy in United Methodism is an episcopacy fully responsible to the General, Jurisdictional, and Central conferences of the church. Whatever may have been an apparently privileged status of the episcopacy in one of the original churches now constituting United Methodism at certain periods in the past, it enjoys no such status today and does not ask for it. It is fully subject to whatever regulations may be adopted by the law-making body of the church; it does not have the privilege of debate or vote in the General Conference; it does not have power of final judicial decision, this being mandated to the Judicial Council; and it is subject to assignment to areas by the Jurisdictional or Central conferences even without consultation, so far as the law is concerned. Each individual bishop is subject to the quadrennial passage of character and administration, and while a bishop may not be deprived of office without trial, the same may be discontinued as a bishop on the effective list if the Jurisdictional Conference deems such discontinuance best either from the viewpoint of the bishop or church. There is much casual talk today about the power of the bishops, but in actual fact, the only real power that any United Methodist bishop has is that which flows out of the example of his life and character, and his demonstrated qualities of church leadership.

All bishops in United Methodism possess exactly the same authority, receive the same salary (allowing for differences in the economy overseas and that in the home field), and possess exactly the same ecclesiastical status. The idea of an archbishop, a presiding bishop, a stated clerk, or a chief denominational executive represents a lodgement of power in a single individual which United Methodism has never been willing to accept.

A General Superintendency

The episcopacy in United Methodism, as has been stated, is a general superintendency. This is one of the unique features of our polity as a church. According to United Methodist theory the bishops constitute a single administrative unit overseeing the temporal and spiritual affairs of the church.

This concept of the episcopacy as a general superintendency has deep roots in United Methodism. Originally in Methodism when the number of bishops was small and the work relatively weak, all the bishops attended every conference session together as far as possible and shared in the conducting of the conference. So strong was this sentiment that when the work grew and the bishops had to distribute the conferences among themselves, over a long period the church refused even to enter into the official General Minutes the name of the particular bishop holding a particular Annual Conference.

In the Methodist Episcopal Church, South, until 1914 usually a different bishop was assigned to hold the conference each year; and in the Methodist Episcopal Church, even after the adoption of the area system, it was required that at least one session of each conference during a quadrennium be held by a bishop other than the one assigned to the area. The Evangelical Church adopted an area system of administration in 1930.

So strong was this concept of a general superintendency in original Methodism that one of the restrictive rules written in 1808 was that the General Conference shall not "destroy the plan of our itinerant general superintendency."

With certain adaptations growing out of present conditions and the size of the church, United Methodism still clings to the pattern of a general superintendency with the Council of Bishops serving as a fully functioning single administrative body.

United Methodist Episcopacy—A Device

United Methodist episcopacy was born as a practical device for meeting the needs of its congregations and prosecuting its mission, and it remains basically that to this day.

In the beginning Wesley assumed personally the full leadership of the Methodist societies. He examined the members, appointed the preachers, conducted the conferences in which he consulted with the preachers, but reserved for himself the right of final decision, mapped the strategy of the movement, and even held title to the property. To many he appeared an autocrat, and such he actually was, but essentially his patterns of action reflected in truth not so much a desire to rule as a great concern for the prosecution of the work. So long as life remained, he personally carried pastoral responsibility for the entire Methodist movement.

Wesley's concern for all the churches or societies was paralleled in America by that of Francis Asbury. From 1784 to his death in 1816, he literally carried the church in America on his own shoulders. Appointed and elected originally a general superintendent, he soon apparently either assumed himself or had assumed for him the title of bishop, but the title carried no connotation beyond that of a certain clearly defined responsibility for the care and oversight of the church. So it has been with Methodist episcopacy ever since.

There would never have been an episcopacy in American Methodism aside from a conviction that such was needed for the sake of the church and its mission. If it had failed as a whole to make effective contribution at this point it would doubtless have been laid aside long ago.

The Episcopacy as Responsibility for the Churches

The episcopacy in United Methodism represents a responsibility with relation to the churches, and the bishop looms up in United Methodism not because of himself, but because the local churches loom up so largely.

The first responsibility of the bishop in United Methodism is to do all he can to provide a ministry for the church. This includes the recruitment, training, and deployment of the ministry. Originally Methodist bishops assumed responsibility personally for recruitment and training. They themselves constantly enlisted men for the ministry, and for long years they prescribed the courses of study. As the church has grown, recruitment and training became a responsibility of other designated agencies of the church, but the bishops still carry a great burden of concern particularly at these points.

The deployment of the ministry is still the bishop's first duty. He must see that every church in his area has a minister, the best trained minister possible. Every church, however small, has the right to look to him for this, and somehow he must find the answer. The one great dread of any true bishop at conference time is to find himself under the necessity of reading out any church however small "to be supplied." Even if he does find himself in such a dilemma he is under obligation to begin the very next day seeking to find a minister for such church. The fact that in almost every Methodist conference when the appointments are read there are no vacant churches, or practically none, is a striking comment upon the episcopacy as a practical device for manning the church.

In order for the episcopacy thus to supply the needs of the churches for a ministry, a Methodist bishop must have available for deployment a group of ministers fully committed to the mission of the church above personal interest. This is what United Methodism asks of all its ministers in the questions propounded before admission into full conference membership and in the ordination vows. This does not mean that in the present day a United Methodist minister is not consulted about his appointment or that he has no freedom of expression of choice— but it does mean that with him the mission must come first.

Furthermore, for the bishop to supply the needs of all the churches necessitates a ministry that is essentially mobile and which can be deployed as a total team to meet a total situation in the life of the church in a given area. The old Methodist term "itinerant" has largely dropped out of use, but the concept and practice of a mobile ministry remains as an essential element in United Methodist polity.

Finally, the United Methodist bishop needs sufficient power to discharge so heavy a responsibility. This is given in what is known as the appointive power. It should be understood that in the granting of such power United Methodism has had in mind not the enhancement of the episcopal office, but the interest of the church. It is true that there have been at times bishops who have been arbitrary in the use of this power, or who at least have given that impression; but the wiser men in the episcopacy have always known that the wisest use of power is to use it sparingly. It should be further understood that in the modern day the appointive power has had certain limitations placed upon it which are calculated to operate for the protection of all concerned. At the same time there is still reserved to the bishop enough freedom in the exercise of the appointing power to enable him to discharge his responsibility.

The Episcopacy as Responsibility for the Ministry

While United Methodism asks much of its ministers in the ordination vows, at the same time it assumes a responsibility for them that few churches assume.

This responsibility for the placement of every minister is made the direct responsibility of the bishop. The bishop is under obligation to find some place even for the person who is not in demand in the churches.

Ultimately the bishop becomes the minister's protection against developing situations which cannot be handled; against too long continuance in one field because of the lack of a call elsewhere, and against the tyranny of local officials and members who would sometimes limit the full freedom of the pulpit.

The Episcopacy as Responsibility for Inspiring the Church

It has not always been realized that what United Methodism actually has asked of its episcopacy first of all is that it be a continuing source of inspiration to its preachers and people. The truly great bishops of the church across the years have been those who have had the capacity to inspire. Such capacity to inspire has always rooted primarily in what they were as individuals, possessed of obvious integrity, reflecting the radiance of Christian experience, and giving themselves with holy abandon to the work. Furthermore, such bishops have been able to inspire the church by their preaching, their writing, their sensitivity to issues in the life of the church and society, and their ability to take positive leadership in the planning of church's strategy.

It cannot be claimed that all United Methodist bishops have measured up to this expectation upon the part of the church or that all who have shown some capacity to inspire have been equally effective. Nevertheless, United Methodism continues to look to its bishops to have at least something in common with an effective field marshal able both to command and inspire his troops.

A Constitutional Episcopacy

United Methodists have always felt free to criticize the episcopacy, and at times they have put new curbs upon it; yet they have held on to it and continue so to do. This is not because of any great reverence for the episcopacy as such, but because of an acceptance of its functional role in meeting the needs of the church.

The episcopacy in United Methodism is protected by the Restrictive Rules which provide that "The General Conference shall not change or alter any part or rule of our government so as to do away with episcopacy or destroy the plan of our itinerant general superintendency" (Article III, Paragraph 17). To change this provision of the law would require a two-thirds vote in both the General Conference and the Annual Conferences. Furthermore there is the provision that the council shall "plan for the general oversight and promotion of the temporal and spiritual interests of the entire Church" (Paragraph 52).

The exact meaning of this time-honored provision has never been spelled out by the General Conference or interpreted by the Judicial Council.

Likewise, the meaning of the term "do away with episcopacy" in the Restrictive Rules has not been a subject of debate in our own time, although it was often debated in the past. The original wording of the rule in The Methodist Church written in 1808 was "do away episcopacy." In the *Discipline* of The United Methodist Church the change is made to the words "do away with episcopacy." The question has been asked by some whether there was actually any alteration made in the rule as originally written by adding the word "with." However that may be, the wording now stands officially in The United Methodist Church as "do away with episcopacy."

There has occurred in the church across the years a gradual modifying of the episcopacy, but generally speaking it may be observed that placing certain reasonable limitations upon the episcopacy has not been interpreted in any significant sense as "doing away with episcopacy."

The Individual Bishop

Each United Methodist bishop is elected by either a Jurisdictional or a Central Conference. Election is by ballot, without nomination by whatever majority the electing body may determine. Usually this figure is fixed at from sixty to sixty-six and two-thirds present.

A person to be eligible for election as a bishop must be an ordained elder. A bishop from some other Jurisdictional or Central Conference is appointed by the Council of Bishops to share in the consecration of each bishop elected. The purpose of this is to symbolize that a bishop is consecrated a bishop of the entire church and not just a bishop of a Jurisdictional or Central Conference.

While in the Jurisdictional Conferences election is for life, in some of the Central Conferences election is for a term only. The reason for this alternative arrangement is that in some Central Conferences there are only one or two bishops, and the situation needs therefore to be kept more flexible. A few Central Conferences have, however, chosen life episcopacy, and, in at least two, election is possible for life after an initial term of service which has been judged satisfactory.

The individual bishop is assigned to a particular area by the Jurisdictional or Central Conference. Assignment is subject to review every four years by the Committee on Episcopacy and by the assigning Jurisdictional or Central Conference. In the jurisdiction the bishop may not be assigned to the same area for longer than a twelve-year period. Within the particular area the individual bishop represents the supreme administrative power of the church.

Retirement comes for the individual bishop at the Jurisdictional Conference preceding his seventy-second birthday.

A process is provided for the transferring of a bishop from one jurisdiction to another, but up to date, use has not been made of this legislation.

The responsibilities of the individual bishop within his episcopal area include caring for all the churches, traveling throughout the area, presiding in the Annual Conference sessions, fixing the appointments of the preachers, choosing the district superintendents, fixing charge and district boundaries, and seeing that the entire program of the church is promoted and that the law of the church is duly administered. In addition to these general duties the *Discipline* spells out in much detail an almost endless number of routine administrative responsibilities which are assigned to the bishop in charge.

The bishops of each Jurisdictional or Central Conference, both active and retired, constitute the College of Bishops of that particular unit. They meet together periodically for counsel and for planning the work within the Jurisdictional or Central Conference.

The Bishops as a Company

Within The United Methodist Church and its predecessor churches since 1784 some four hundred men have been elected to the episcopacy. They have represented a wide variety of types and have been marked by sundry gifts. Some of them have been primarily pulpit giants, some administrators, some educators, some church lawyers, some evangelists, some writers, and some teachers. Some of them have been conservatives and some of them liberals. Some have been bishops whose influence and leadership have been church wide, and others have been bishops who have majored upon the particular area assignment that has been theirs. All in all they have been a company of devoted men who have sought to discharge faithfully the work to which the church called them. A number of them have actually died on the road in the discharge of their duties, in some cases far, far away from home. It was so with the first two bishops—Bishop Coke who died at sea and Bishop Asbury who died en route trying desperately to make his way to the General Conference of 1816. Bishops Seybert, George, Emory, Fitzgerald, Kingsley, Thompson, Wiley, Bascom, and

Tigert in an earlier day and Bishops Leonard, Garth, Baxter, Middleton, and Gregory in our own day all died on the road.

Only four of this large company of bishops chose to resign the office. One of these, Bishop Fisher, resigned to return to the pastorate, and Bishop Hamline resigned because of his conviction that the holding of episcopal status should not be for life.

The honor of being a bishop for the longest number of years belonged to Bishop Herbert Welch who lived to the age of one hundred six and was a bishop for fifty-two years.

In late years an earlier retirement age has been fixed, and a number of men have been elected late in life. As a result the average length of active service for bishops elected since Methodist union in 1939 has been slightly better than ten years.

The Council of Bishops

From the beginning, the Council of Bishops and its predecessors—the Board of Bishops of the Methodist Episcopal Church, the College of Bishops of the Methodist Episcopal Church, South, and the Board of Bishops of the Evangelical United Brethren Church—have played a primary role in the life of the church.

The Council of Bishops is composed of all the bishops of the church, active and retired, and meets twice each year. Its officers include a president who serves for one year, a president-designate, and a secretary who serves by the quadrennium. It seeks to do its work through an executive committee, and certain major work committees which include all members of the council. These are at present the Committee on Administration, the Committee on Pastoral Concerns, the Committee on Teaching, and the Committee on Relationships.

As of this writing the council includes sixty bishops in the active relationship, forty-five serving areas in the United States and fifteen serving areas in other parts of the world. It also includes forty-nine bishops who have retired.

By its very nature the Council of Bishops has been and is a medium contributing to the church's unity and a cohesive force that holds the church together. In its membership every geographic part of the church and every interest of the denomination find continuing representation. The composition of the General Conference meeting only once every four years changes significantly with each session, but because of life episcopacy coupled with quadrennial retirements and elections, the composition of the Council of Bishops is characterized by periodic renewal, but at the same time meaningful continuity. Older bishops retire and new men are elected, but there is always a nucleus of ongoing, but constantly changing leadership in the council. Not only by its representative nature as a body, but much more by its natural collective concern for the "care of all the churches," the Council of Bishops contributes continuously and significantly to the togetherness of the church.

The bishops have had historically, and the Council of Bishops continues to have, an important teaching role in the life of the church. The bishops quite properly are expected to be custodians of the faith, exemplifying it, defending it, and sharing it effectively with all for whom they have responsibility.

An interesting acknowledgment of this is found in the

original association of the bishops with the Publishing House founded in 1789 as the first general agency created by the church to extend the faith. Because this was the primary function of the Publishing House, the bishops were closely associated with it, editing the *Discipline* at first and apparently having strong influence in determining what should be published and distributed. A vestige of this early relationship still survives, though the original reason is generally overlooked, in the custom yet followed by the Publishing House of supplying the bishops with copies of the various works and publications which it produces.

Just as the Council of Bishops is expected to exercise a teaching role at the level of the general church, so also is the individual bishop expected to exercise a teaching role at the level of his own area.

Through its periodic meetings the Council of Bishops affords opportunity for regular consultation by the respective area administrators regarding the ongoing concerns of the church and likewise upon new developments affecting the life of the church. This process makes possible planning for necessary follow-through at the area and Annual Conference level. Through this regular consultation the Council of Bishops attempts to meet the obligation laid upon it by the *Discipline* to "plan for the general oversight and promotion of the temporal and spiritual interests of the entire Church" and "to promote the evangelistic activities of the church, and furnish such inspirational leadership as the need and opportunity may demand."

The Council of Bishops likewise has responsibility for seeing that certain mechanics of church administration are cared for properly. Just as the bishop holding an Annual Conference session is responsible for seeing that all proper business of the conference is cared for before final adjournment, so the bishops as a body have a similar responsibility for the church as a whole. These mechanics of administration include such matters as perfecting the plan of episcopal visitation, providing for the episcopal administration of units not embraced in Jurisdictional or Central conferences, or of episcopal areas in case of a death in the active episcopal ranks and making certain nominations. The reasoning back of the lodging of certain nominating responsibility in the Council of Bishops is the fact that here every part of the church and every member has a representative at court.

The bishops collectively have two chief ways of addressing the church.

The first of these is by way of the Episcopal Address to the General Conference, the presenting of which has been customary since 1812. This address is presented at or near the opening of the General Conference session. It is prepared and read by one of the bishops chosen by vote of the council. It is reviewed in detail by the whole council and thus becomes a genuinely collective document. It is signed individually by all the bishops except as anyone of them might for reasons sufficient to himself see fit not to sign it. This has happened only rarely.

The other way by which the bishops collectively address the church is by the issuance of occasional messages coming out of the meetings of the Council of Bishops. These deal with subjects particularly pertinent at a particular hour in the life of the church and of the world.

Furthermore it has long been customary to allow the bishops to address episcopal greetings to the church with each issue of the *Discipline*. These are to be found at the beginning of each volume.

According to United Methodist law the Council of Bishops is given no authority to act for the church between sessions of the General Conference, neither is it given any power of control over the Annual Conferences or over the various agencies of the church. There are always those who want it to act to censor some board, seek to remove an editor, reject a position taken by some agency, or take some other action in which such persons are particularly interested. This insistence comes equally from conservatives and liberals. Strange to say those who thus urge the council to act or speak do this only with reference to positions which they themselves endorse. Should it act or speak otherwise, they quickly join the critics of what is called "episcopal power." But the Council of Bishops is given no such authority. It can act and speak only for itself with such weight as its own words and actions may carry. The council is not a control body in United Methodism. It should be understood that back of this limitation lies almost two hundred years of history. Long ago Methodism decided that no one, including the bishops, can act finally for the church except the General Conference itself, and in some cases only the entire church by constitutional vote in all the Annual Conferences.

The members of the Council of Bishops do not participate in the General Conference sessions except as observers and presiding officers. It was otherwise, however, in the Evangelical United Brethren Church. The Methodist Church long ago removed its bishops from floor participation with the adoption of the delegated General Conference. There are now those outside the bishops who think that the present procedure immobilizes needed leadership and that the present practice should be further reviewed.

The Council of Bishops carries weight in the life of the church. Such weight as is carried can root ultimately, however, only in what the bishops are as persons and what they produce as those who compose the council. True leadership can never be granted. It has to be achieved. While certain persons are elected to the episcopal office from time to time, they actually become bishops indeed only as they prove themselves effective servants of the church at the episcopal level.

The church has always looked to the bishops to afford a measure of balance in the life of the church as a whole. How this responsibility for affording a measure of balance has been spelled out has changed with the years. At one time it involved the power to arrest the acts of the General Conference or to pass upon their constitutionality. All this now belongs to the past. At the present, however, some vestige of this responsibility is still to be found in the *Discipline's* provision for a majority of the Council of Bishops to request the Judicial Council to determine the constitutionality of any act of the General Conference.

Although the church from time to time has changed the law as to exactly how this responsibility of the episcopacy at the point of providing balance is to be discharged, it has always expected and still expects its bishops to help the church to keep its head and not be stampeded into hasty and unwise action, or breaking with its traditions or time-tested practices without being at least fully aware of the implications of any break which it may be considering.

Among the oldest words in the *Discipline* are those which list it as the duty of a bishop "to oversee the spiritual and temporal affairs of the Church." This does not inply that the individual bishop or the bishops as a group should dictate to the church, and no bishop worthy of the office would desire to. It does imply, however, that the bishops are expected to carry a banner and set an example of integrity and devotion and creative imagination. No right-thinking person will be too critical of such a role conscientiously and respectfully played.

The Episcopal Insignia

The bishops of The United Methodist Church have an official insignia which they wear upon their robes and sometimes use upon their stationery and in other appropriate ways. It was taken over from the former Evangelical United Brethren Church. Its colors are red and gold and silver on a black background, and it includes the cross, the alpha and omega, and the shepherd's staff formed by the Greek letters chi and rho symbolizing the lordship of Christ. It speaks appropriately of the responsibility of the bishop to be a faithful shepherd of the flock of Christ.

Much has been written about the episcopacy in the United Brethren, the Evangelical, and the Methodist traditions, but perhaps no one ever summed up more tersely what the episcopacy in United Methodism is intended to be and ought to be, than did the pioneer bishop of a century ago, Bishop Robert R. Roberts, who is reported to have said, "Methodist bishops should be distinguished by the greatness of their devotion and the simplicity of their wants."

VIII

The Concept of the District Superintendency

The district superintendency in United Methodism represents the chief way by which the connectionalism of the church is maintained and made effective. So far as the local churches are concerned the superintendent is, in a very real sense, the connectionalism. He comes regularly into each local church, and his visits become the chief point of contact of that particular church, be it large or small with The United Methodist Church as a whole.

The contact of the district superintendent with the local church comes to sharpest focus in the Charge Conference over which he presides. Here the connectionalism is localized, and the presence and presiding of the district superintendent strongly dramatize the fact that the Charge Conference is the connecting link between the local and general churches. Here church officers are elected, and here general oversight of the administrative board is lodged. Here final decision is made regarding property matters and concerning the response of the local church to the financial calls of the larger church.

Regularly in the Charge Conference, and in special meetings and personal interviews, the district superintendent presents the claims and interests and concerns of the larger church. In turn, in the cabinet, in conference with the bishop, and in the church at large the superintendent becomes the advocate of the local churches of the district and represents their concerns as they have been shared with him.

There are more than five hundred district superintendents in The United Methodist Church. They blanket every foot of territory in the United States and vast areas in other countries where United Methodism operates. They keep in contact continually with every congregation and are available for counsel with every preacher and lay person. They are the living links by which the connectionalism is kept alive and functioning with efficiency.

Development of the Office

The district superintendency in United Methodism developed originally as a device to meet a particular situation obtaining at the time. The earliest name given to the office was that of "presiding elder." For long years the office was known in both the Methodist Episcopal Church and the Methodist Episcopal Church, South, by this name. At Methodist union in 1939 the term "district superintendent" was officially approved for the office.

When The Methodist Church in America was formally organized in 1784 John Wesley indicated his desire that no more elders should be ordained than were absolutely necessary and that the work on the continent should be divided among them. The organizing conference therefore elected and consecrated twelve elders for this purpose. Their function was to supervise the work, help the unordained men, and administer the sacraments. The plan proved so effective that shortly the number was increased beyond the original twelve. Gradually the office of "presiding elder" came into being, largely inspired by this original plan for making the sacraments available. The custom of having the communion in connection with the visit of the presiding elder traces back ultimately to the day when the number of ordained ministers was limited.

The General Conference of 1792 approved the office officially and spelled out its nature and duties. The term "presiding elder" was used in the Methodist Episcopal Church until 1908 when it was changed to "district superintendent." It was retained in the Methodist Episcopal Church, South, until the time of Methodist union in 1939.

The churches in the Evangelical United Brethren tradition had a similar office. At the time of union in 1968 the term employed by them was "conference superintendent." Each Annual Conference had one or more such superintendents depending upon its size.

Assistant to the Bishop

It is always to be remembered that in United Methodist polity the district superintendent is first of all an assistant to the bishop. Theoretically the bishop does have responsibility for the care of all the churches of his assigned area, but because United Methodist episcopal areas are so large, as compared for instance with a diocese in the Protestant Episcopal Church, the bishop is given the district superintendents as assistants within particular geographic territories. Every district superintendent is the bishop's man so far as his district is concerned. This does not mean that he is not to be a fully free man having the right to his own opinions and at liberty to disagree with the bishop if necessary, but it does mean that he represents the bishop within the territory assigned him and that whatever problems become the bishop's within his district automatically become his problems also. Furthermore it is to be remembered that while he is assigned to a particular district, he is not just the superintendent of that particular district, but rather one of the superintendents of the entire conference. He has no moral or legal right to attempt to build a fence about his district. All the problems of the conference are his problems, too, because in the end they all belong to the bishop, and as one of the bishop's assistants he must willingly carry his proper share of them.

It may well be pointed out at this juncture that United Methodist polity accords to the bishop the right to choose the district superintendents. There are those who object to this and would like to see the superintendents chosen by some other method. Parenthetically it may be observed that it is scarcely less logical to allow the bishops to choose the persons who are to work most intimately with them than to accord to pastors the privilege of choosing staff members who are to work with them. Very early in Methodism there was a strong demand for the election of presiding elders, but this thinking did not prevail. It reappeared from time to time, but this position was never adopted in The Methodist Church. The Evangelical United Brethren Church did follow the custom of electing conference superintendents. In The United Methodist Church the pattern followed in The Methodist Church prevails, and the bishops are left free to choose their district superintendents. Most of them today, however, do not exercise this right without conference with other persons both clerical and lay whose judgments may be helpful to them in making their choices.

The Cabinet

As the bishop's representative within a given area the district superintendent becomes a member of the bishop's cabinet. Interestingly enough while the cabinet is referred to frequently in the *Discipline,* and has been for a century and a half and more, it is not actually defined in so many words although its various duties are spelled out again and yet again. On the basis of tradition and long practice the cabinet of each Annual Conference is composed of the bishop and the respective district superintendents.

The number of districts in a given conference is determined by the Annual Conference itself. Once the number is set, it is the responsibility of the bishop to fix the district boundaries.

All cabinets meet frequently throughout the year on many matters, but obviously the most dramatic work of the cabinet is the making of the appointments. There was a time in an earlier day when a bishop might consult as he desired with the cabinet and then proceed to make the appointments alone if he chose to do so, and there were some so-called "Bourbon bishops" who once followed this practice. It was in reaction to this procedure that legislation was finally adopted providing that the bishop must share his final list of appointments with the cabinet before reading them to the conference. This, of course, seems like a strange Disciplinary provision to those who do not know the long story that lies behind it.

Today all bishops make the fullest use of their cabinets in appointment making, and back of every set of appointments there lie long hours of consultation with both churches and ministers and diligent labor in cabinet sessions to complete a total set of appointments which deploy the total ministry of the conference in such a way as to meet the total needs of all the churches of the conference. Each bishop develops his own cabinet methods, and most bishops in the present day are open to changes in such methods as the time and occasion may seem to warrant. When a given set of appointments is finally completed, they are of necessity the bishop's appointments for which he must be willing to assume full responsibility. Though the opinion of all the cabinet members is sought diligently there is properly no such thing under United Methodist polity as determination of an appointment by majority vote of the cabinet. The final decision regarding every appointment is in the end with the bishop presiding over the Annual Conference.

Relation to Churches and Pastors

One of the chief functions of the district superintendents as assistant to the bishop is to be a counselor to the pastors and people and churches of the district. The carrying out of this responsibility will occupy the larger portion of one's time and energies. It will involve constant traveling of the district, multiplied interviews, and a heavy volume of correspondence.

So far as the churches of the district are concerned, this function of the district superintendent will involve doing what is essentially a development job. One of the chief responsibilities of the district superintendent is to help all the churches of the district become what they can be and ought to be. Accomplishing this end will call for creative imagination, hard labor, and continuing devotion. It will involve constant counseling with the churches regarding goals and how best to achieve them, almost endless interviews with individuals and committees, the distribution of helpful literature and other resource material, and the arrangement of wisely planned district and zone meetings to afford knowledge of promising methods for the improvement of church operation as well as inspiration to undertake them. Doing a genuine development job with the churches of the district calls for the superintendent to take a positive and imaginative lead and to lift up a banner to which the people may rally.

So far as the pastors of the district are concerned the function of the district superintendent as counselor will involve counseling with them in pastors' meetings as may be necessary, but particularly individually. Rather than waiting for his pastors to seek him out the effective district superintendent will find ways and means to take the initiative in creating opportunities for counseling. Especially will he counsel with the pastors regarding the effectiveness of their own ministry and the things that make for its enrichment or detract from its effectiveness. Furthermore the district superintendent is responsible for counseling with the pastors regarding problems that arise in the field of church administration in the parish to which the pastor is assigned. Especially is this to be done with the younger ministers who feel the need of the accumulated wisdom that only experience in the ministry can bring.

The district superintendent is to be, however, more than just a counselor to the pastors of the district. He is to be a pastor and a shepherd to them and to their families. He is the only pastor that these persons and their families have. Parsonage homes are not exempt from the tensions and frustrations and even tragedies that other homes experience. Only in late years has there been a frank and realistic acknowledgement of this, and out of this realization some

Annual Conferences have established effective counseling services for ministers and their families. All this serves but to dramatize the need for the district superintendent to be a genuine pastor to the pastors of the district.

Likewise the district superintendent is definitely charged with being a counselor with both churches and pastors regarding the appointments. When it is felt that there is need for a change in appointment he is charged to counsel with those responsible as to how serious this need is, what type of pastor the church needs if a change is to be made, and if it is desired, concerning certain ministers who might well be considered for such appointment. In turn the district superintendent is to counsel with the pastor concerning his or her possible placement for another year. Following these counseling sessions the district superintendent represents both churches and pastors in the cabinet and in conference with the bishop. It is to be noted, however, that while the *Discipline* provides that the district superintendent shall counsel with both churches and pastors, it does not go beyond that. What is received in such interviews is judged to be simply advice for what it may prove to be worth. Final decision under United Methodist polity still lies with the bishop. It should be observed, however, that no bishop and no cabinet in the church as we know it today would fail to take with greatest seriousness the recommendations of either church or pastor even though in the end they might not be able to go along with them.

Like the bishop, the district superintendent as the bishop's assistant is responsible for laying upon the hearts of the churches the concerns of United Methodism as a whole. This job in a very real sense is a promotional job. United Methodism as a church has a concern for evangelism, for reaching persons and leading them to become disciples. The district superintendent therefore has a responsibility to promote evangelism. United Methodism as a church has a concern for Christian education to see those who have become disciples grow in the Christian life. The district superintendent therefore has a responsibility for Christian education involving the growth and effectiveness of the church school, the use of United Methodist curriculum material, and the provisions for training opportunities and experiences.

United Methodism as a church has a concern for a truly Christian society. The district superintendent therefore has a responsibility to help the churches and people of his district think through the social implications of the gospel for the present day, and to this end it is his privilege to seek to involve them in study and social action.

United Methodism as a church has a vast program of activity which is worldwide in its scope and which is supported through World Service. The district superintendent therefore has a responsibility to promote World Service which represents the very base line of all the far-flung activities of the church as a whole.

In addition, United Methodism has a concern for many special causes which merit the full support of the church such as higher education, Advance specials, ministerial education, black colleges, and human relations projects. The General Conference has made clear and thoughtful decisions regarding all these causes. The district superintendent therefore has a responsibility to promote all of them.

In addition to promoting the causes of the general church the district superintendent has also the responsibility to promote causes officially approved by the Jurisdictional Conference and the Annual Conference.

There are today those both among the ministry and

the laity who take exception to the very idea of promotion, to say nothing of questionable methods of promotion. Suffice it to say, however, that nothing worth accomplishing is achieved without effort, and a church the size of United Methodism cannot play the full role it should in a day such as our own aside from the legitimate promotion of the securing of necessary financial resources. The busience superintendents, in making their rounds has been, around the calling of certain questions. One of the questions most frequently called by the district superintendents, or before them the presiding elders, or the conference superintendents, in making their rounds has been, "What has been done for?" Then has followed the listing of some cause such as missions, Christian education, World Service, or any one of a number of other causes dear to the church. Without apology United Methodism has always summoned her churches and people to glad response to such causes, and she will continue to do so, so long as she remains true to her heritage as a concerned church.

A Power Position

Without question the district superintendency in United Methodism is, by its very nature, a power position. It is for this reason that it has come under sharp attack at times, and that there have been periodic efforts to alter it. There have been those from time to time, as there are now, who have advocated doing away with the office altogether. More generally, however, the effort has been to abridge its power by legislation and to provide that the same person shall not occupy the office for too long a time. In earlier years there was a time limit upon the number of years a member of conference might serve upon a given district, but not upon the number of years one might serve in the office itself. The result was that some ministers rotated from one district to another and thus became perpetuals in the office. The unforgettable Peter Cartwright, for instance, completed fifty years as a presiding elder, establishing what was probably a record. For some years now there has stood in the *Discipline* a provision that makes rotation in the office necessary. The present provision is that a minister may serve as district superintendent no more than six years out of nine.

Because of its nature, the district superintendency will continue a topic of general conversation among United Methodists for a long time to come, and attempts will continue to be made from time to time to change it in various ways. So long as it remains as a vital part of United Methodist polity it will continue to be a power position. Some who fall heir to it may abuse its power. Honesty forces admission that some have done so in the past, and a few will probably continue to do so. But more thoughtful and devoted persons appointed to it, knowing full well that it is a power position, will refuse to treat it so and will in all sincerity and humility insist upon regarding themselves as only the servants of the servants of Christ.

IX

The Concept of the Laity

While the ordained ministry looms largely in United Methodism and represents a basic pillar in its ecclesiastical structure, the heart of United Methodism is to be found in its laity, the multiplied thousands of men, women, young people, and children who constitute its membership and constituency.

United Methodism began largely as a lay movement. Such early leaders as John and Charles Wesley, Thomas Coke, and Philip Otterbein were ordained clergymen, but most of the preachers were at first lay preachers, and it was around the labors of these that the leaders structured the early progress of the work. United Methodism's first places of worship, particularly in the United States, were often the homes of its people. The references in the diaries and correspondence of the early preachers relative to their preaching schedules mention over and over again family names, such as that of Judge White in Delaware or Henry Gough in Maryland or John Durham in Kentucky or of Edward Cox in east Tennessee or of Governor Van Cortlandt in New York.

Oftentimes it was lay persons who on their own anticipated the arrival of the appointed missionary and laid the foundations of the church. Such was the case in New York City where Philip Embury and Barbara Heck, lay persons, began Methodist work in advance of the coming of the emissaries of John Wesley; and the same was true in Maryland where a lay preacher, Robert Strawbridge, began the initial work. These first Methodists having been converted in one place, would move into a new section and, carrying their religion with them, would begin meetings for fellowship and worship and then request the services of a minister. The full story of the work of lay persons in planting the church has never been adequately told. It involves many interesting and fascinating characters indeed such as Green Hill, a layman of large means who helped plant the church in both North Carolina and Tennessee, or Madame Russell, the sister of Patrick Henry, whose home was an early center of the work in southwest Virginia.

Yet despite the fact that Methodism originally was in many important respects a lay movement, in the United States it remained in fact very largely a preacher's church for roughly the first one hundred years of its existence. Annual Conferences were made up of ministers alone as was also the General Conference. At one time the Annual Conferences even met behind closed doors for their business sessions, but did allow the laity to share in the public preaching services that were scheduled as something of a side feature of the conference itself. The early history of the United Brethren Church and the Evangelical Association followed essentially the same pattern.

THE CONCEPT OF THE LAITY

The Class Leader

The passing years have been marked in United Methodism by an ever-increasing involvement of the laity in the total life of the church. This process began with the provision for lay leadership in the local society. This was the class leader. This lay person was chosen for evident piety and devotion, and was truly the undershepherd for the group that he was appointed to serve. He watched over them in love, conducted the class meeting, encouraged their testimony, and collected their gifts for the society. What the class leaders actually did for the building up of Methodism especially in the first one hundred years is a story known fully only to God.

In due time the class leaders passed from the stage, and other local lay church officers took their place as the pattern of local church operation changed with the years. These were stewards, trustees, Sunday school superintendents and officers and teachers, members of the Administrative Board, lay leaders, superintendents of study, and committee chairpersons and members too numerous to mention.

Lay Ministers

Another use of lay persons dating back to the beginning is represented by the lay preacher. United Methodism in all its predecessor branches employed lay preachers from the beginning. Very early the term "local preacher" began to be used in Methodism. The term "local preacher" has now passed from United Methodist vocabulary, but what it once represented needs to be understood if our history is to be appreciated fully. In Methodism in the early days, and until only a few years ago, local preachers were of two classes. First of all they were former members of the Annual Conferences who for health or family reasons had been forced to desist from traveling and were therefore located voluntarily by the conference. As located preachers they maintained their ministerial credentials, but functioned only where they lived, preaching and otherwise serving as opportunity afforded.

The other type of local preacher was the duly licensed layman, who took certain studies and sometimes went on to be ordained a local deacon or elder. Such a person did not join the conference, but preached near home as opportunity afforded and on occasion even supplied a small charge for which no regularly appointed minister was available. In isolated sections he often performed marriages and buried the dead. At one time the number of these local preachers mounted into the thousands, and they served a highly helpful role especially in remote communities. Today the local preacher of this type is no longer provided for in the *Discipline,* and the number of those who remain of a once great host grows smaller each year as one by one they pass from labor to rest.

The present-day successors of the former local preacher are the lay pastor, who now serves so many of the smaller charges of United Methodism, and the lay speaker who gladly gives his or her witness as occasion may demand.

The *Discipline* now provides also for what is known as the lay worker. This is a person other than the clergy who makes a career of employment by the church or church agencies. Such lay worker must meet certain standards, is related to the Conference Committee on the Lay Worker, and is eligible for consecration at the Annual Conference. He or she has the privilege of being seated in the conference with voice but not vote.

THE CONCEPT OF THE LAITY

Lay Representation

Lay representation in the Annual and General conferences, now so familiar a pattern in United Methodism, was a long, long time in coming, and it is difficult today to imagine how bitter a battle had to be fought for such representation finally to be obtained. The early efforts looking in the direction of laity rights met with such strong resistance that the final result was the first serious division in American Methodism coming in 1828 and resulting in the formation of the Methodist Protestant Church. It is often overlooked that this drama of the first strong struggle for laity rights was played out against the background of the Jacksonian era in the life of the country, and the struggle in the nation for full democracy beyond doubt had overtones for the structure of the church.

Lay representation in the General Conference was not voted, however, in the Methodist Episcopal Church, South, until 1866, in the Methodist Episcopal Church until 1868, in the United Brethren Church until 1888, and in the Evangelical Association until 1903. At first this was not fully balanced lay representation in some cases. Lay representation in the Annual Conference came in 1866 in the Methodist Episcopal Church, South, in 1877 in the United Brethren Church, and in the Evangelical Association in 1907. In the case of the Methodist Episcopal Church it did not come until as late as 1932. At first in some cases there was only token lay representation from each district. It was not until Methodist union in 1939 that for Methodism lay representation in the Annual Conference was assured to each and every pastoral charge. The Methodist Protestant Church always had full lay representation at all levels, this having been a basic issue in its establishment.

Today conscientious effort continues to seek to insure an adequate proportion of lay delegates in the Annual Conference. This concern is reflected in the current legislation which provides for a multiple number of lay delegates to the Annual Conferences from local churches sufficiently large to have a multiple clergy staff, and also that which provides that an Annual Conference may develop a formula of its own to guarantee that the number of lay representatives to the Annual Conference matches the number of clerical members.

A still further protection of the voice of the laity in the church from the viewpoint of many persons is the provision that in the General Conference a vote by orders may be called for by two-thirds of either the laity or the clergy. Upon the invoking of this rule a majority vote of each order is necessary for any motion to prevail. The rule is seldom invoked, but it does stand as an added protection, particularly for the lay side of the house in General Conference which sees itself as representing the great body of the rank and file membership of the total church. On the other hand, the clerical side of the General Conference is elected by a far smaller group of persons, namely the clergy of the church, and could on occasion conceivably represent perhaps too strongly the clerical mind.

Recognition of Women

The struggle for the recognition of women in the church required a still longer period of time. For a number of years the position was taken officially that the provisions for lay representation in the General and Annual conferences did not apply to women. Test cases were made, some of them involving individuals as well known as the famous Frances E. Willard, as to whether women could be elected and seated as lay representatives in the General Conference. These test cases met with strong resistance from some quarters, but eventually the battle for full laity rights for women was won in the Methodist Episcopal Church in 1900 and in the Methodist Episcopal Church, South, in 1922. The establishment of full laity rights for women at the General Conference and Annual Conference level carried with it the establishment of the right to hold local church office. The admission of women into the traveling ministry did not come in Methodism until some years later.

Likewise, official General Conference recognition of organizations for women of the church also met with resistance at first, but this recognition came eventually in the eighteen seventies or eighties. The struggle for this recognition was led by such women as Frances Willard, Belle Harris Bennett, Mary Helm, Lizzie Hoffman Derickson, and others, and all too often the opposition was led by some of the bishops of the church.

Recognition of Youth

The need to recognize the young adults and youth of the church came to sharp focus as late as our own day. This does not mean that the predecessor churches of United Methodism in earlier years were indifferent to young people. Rather these churches loved them and sought to help them by developing various organizations for them such as the Sunday school, the Epworth League, Christian Endeavor, and the United Methodist Youth Fellowship. This pattern was followed particularly in the period beginning about 1890 and continuing until only recently.

Today, however, a new idea has come to grip the thinking of the church to the effect that not only should good things be done *for* young people, but that they should also be done *with* young people, and therefore young people should be radically involved in the total ongoing life of the church and thus allowed to make their own possible contribution. To this end, previous legislation has been eliminated from the *Discipline* which set a minimum age for membership in the Annual, Jurisdictional, and General conferences and in the Judicial Council. Furthermore the legislation for the general agencies of the church has been rewritten as to assure adequate representation of the younger life of the church at every important point of decision.

Minorities

Another late development in the role of the laity of the church is that represented by the current legislation and practice designed to insure that all minorities of The United Methodist Church are fully and adequately represented at every level of the church's life. Many of these minority representatives must of necessity be lay persons. Ethnic minorities to which such representation is due are easily identifiable such as blacks, Indians, Oriental Americans, and Spanish Americans. But there are other minorities also who likewise deserve larger representation in the counsels of the church than they now enjoy, such as the rural poor, laborers, farmers, small-town residents, and white city tenement dwellers. Devising ways and means for the accomplishment of such representation is no easy assignment and calls for still further enlightened imagination than as yet has been brought into play in the life of the church. Likewise, United Methodism must still struggle with the problem of how to afford representation particularly to lay persons who represent theological and social viewpoints which may not accord with prevailing general trends in church thinking, but who are nevertheless still a part of the fellowship and therefore deserving of a respectful hearing.

Women's Work

Although statistics are not available, it has probably always been true that women represent a majority of the membership of the local churches. It was a woman, his remarkable mother, who beyond all doubt represented the strongest human influence in determining the character and thinking of John Wesley; and through him Susanna Wesley left her imprint upon the Methodist movement for all the years to come. Some of the most effective help which Wesley and Otterbein and Albright had was that of women who, though not holding formal office, gave significant personal leadership in the local societies. In the era of the high tide of revivalism in the last century there were in the churches of what is now United Methodism women evangelists, some of whom became nationally known such as Phoebe Palmer of the Methodist Episcopal Church and Davila Kring of the Evangelical Church, the mother of Daniel Poling.

Perhaps the greatest contribution of a particular group of women to the total life of the church has been that of the countless host of women Sunday school teachers who across a century and a half, in churches large and small, have devotedly and conscientiously sought to share the faith and bring pupils to know him whom to know aright is life eternal.

The number of various types of organizations for women, both local and churchwide, that have come into being as the years have passed is beyond exact determination. These have included foreign missionary societies, home missionary societies, parsonage and church extension societies, Ladies' Aids, young women's missionary societies, guilds, and other groupings. Today, United Methodist Women represents one of the strongest and most effective church organizations for women anywhere in the world.

Men's Work

Formal organization of men's work in United Methodism came far later than formal organization of women's work or work with young people. Generally it began in the period of the nineteen twenties, although there were sporadic and scattered efforts prior to that time. Conference and district lay organizations were developed, and there was provision for overall direction through a Board of Lay Activities or similar general church agency. In due time efforts were made at the establishment of laymen's clubs in local churches and sometimes at district or zone levels. Such efforts have met with measured response, but as yet lay organizations for men have not met with the degree of success or effectiveness of lay organizations for women or for young people. Perhaps one reason is that in the earlier days of the movement the emphasis was too largely upon the supportive role of the laymen in the life of the church. Hope for continuing improvement in the situation is found in the fact that now this pattern of thinking has undergone considerable change, and the current emphasis is upon fuller participaton of the laity in the total life of the church rather than upon the earlier role of simply "serving tables" and undergirding the ministry in its efforts.

THE CONCEPT OF THE LAITY

All to Be Ministers

United Methodism today in line with its original emphasis upon the laity accepts with enthusiasm the current emphasis popular throughout the religious world upon the idea that ideally every Christian is to be a minister and not simply those who represent the ordained clergy of the church. This idea involves no discounting of the ordained ministry, but rather a lifting of the level of the concept of the laity. Every lay person, as United Methodism sees it, is truly called to ministry and witness even as is the minister. This ministry is to be exercised within and through the channels of the church, but also within the area of one's daily life and work and in the world. This witness is to be given not only by spoken word, but much more by action, by the glad giving of one's resources and oneself, and by attitudes shown in all life's relationships that truly reflect the mind that was in Christ Jesus.

X

The Concept of the Local Church

The connectionalism of United Methodism comes to focus, not in its powerful general boards and agencies, or in its Annual, Jurisdictional, and General conferences, or in its episcopacy, but in its more than forty thousand local churches. It is at this point that the connection becomes most visible.

The *Discipline* defines the local church as a connectional society, and in order that each local church may be an effective connectional unit, makes it the duty of the district superintendents and pastors to organize and administer the charge and local churches in line with the guidance provided by the general church.

United Methodism's local congregations are to be found everywhere in twenty-five countries around the globe. Thousands of them are housed in simple rural chapels set among the trees. Others meet in stately, expensive, imposing edifices which lift up their towers amid the swirl of the busy downtown life of some great city or beside some broad boulevard where the accelerated traffic of the modern day rushes swiftly past. Many are located in new mush-rooming suburban communities, and many still cling to life in neighborhoods that have undergone radical change in character and in a few cases in neighborhoods where people no longer live. Large numbers of these congregations are to be found in smaller cities, villages, crossroads trade centers, and county seat towns. In fact, in the United States at least, that community is seldom to be found where there is not a United Methodist Church of some kind.

These United Methodist local churches differ widely in type. Some of them have only a handful of members, while others number their members by the thousands. Some of them have large resources while others are severely limited at this point. In theory each of these congregations is supposed to represent a cross section of humanity and a place where the rich and poor meet together and God is the Father of all. But in fact, many of them are made up, at least predominantly, of the same type of people such as working-class people, professional and semi-professional people, people of the same ethnic background, or people with like cultural interests.

In theological thinking these United Methodist local churches are as different as they are in other respects. Some are ultraliberal and some are ultraconservative with the others finding their place somewhere in the misty flats that lie between these generally opposing viewpoints.

The local church in United Methodism traces back ultimately to the religious society. A religious society was no more than a group of people organized for a religious purpose, and in United Methodist thinking, a local church is essentially the same thing. The use of the ancient term "society" has long since passed from among us, but the concept of a group of people banded together for a religious purpose still abides in United Methodist thinking concerning the local church.

According to United Methodist thinking the local church exists for mission and for this alone. It is not to be thought of as an end within itself, and as in the case of individuals, it is only when it loses its life that it truly finds it.

To Reach People

The local church according to United Methodist thinking, exists first of all to reach and help people. All people with their fears, their guilt, their sorrows, their sins, their heart hungers, and their deep longing for a redemption which they cannot find in themselves represent a proper concern for every local church. Especially is this true of the people who live within the shadow of each particular local church. As a church United Methodists believe, and have always believed, that numbers are important, not for their own sake and certainly not for the sake of denominational pride, but to the extent that they represent people for whom Christ died. The number in which Jesus seemed to be most interested was the number "one"—one sheep, one coin, one boy—and he reminded his followers that all heaven itself rejoices over just "one sinner that repenteth."

In an earlier day the bishops in all three of the traditions represented in United Methodism asked of the preachers in open conference, "How many conversions have you had this year?" and the welcome news was gladly given and gladly received.

The church is only in line with its heritage across two centuries when without apology it insists that the local church exists to reach people and that when it adds to the fellowship of believers it does the work whereunto God has called it as a church.

To Help People Grow

United Methodists believe furthermore that the local church exists to help people grow spiritually. This was stated specifically in the original outlining of the purpose of the Methodist societies.

The purpose of the local church is to comfort its members, but not to make them comfortable. The word "comfort" as used in the Scriptures carries not just the idea of bringing solace, but rather the idea of strengthening. When the New Testament speaks of "the Comforter" its primary reference is not to one who dries our tears, but rather to one who strengthens our hearts. It is this type of comforting which the local church must provide today.

The purpose of the local church is to challenge its members to a fully Christian conscience, to make them aware of issues now facing the church and society, to help them see the full implications of the gospel for a day like this and to lead them to act responsively.

The purpose of the local church is to cement its members into a community of faith, hope, and love in which all gladly and together seek "to go on to perfection."

A Church in Mission

United Methodism thinks of the local church as existing in and for the world and as the strategic base from which Christians move out to the structures of society. Its ideal for every local church is that it shall be genuinely in mission.

A United Methodist local church may be correctly thought of as truly being in mission when at least five things are true of it.

A local church is in mission when it serves effectively its own immediate constituency. This includes its own members and their families and other persons with whom it has direct contact of some kind. In some quarters it has become somewhat common to discount this function of the local church and to interpret it as the church saving its own life. This judgment is scarcely fair, however. It is true that as Christians grow and mature normally their attachment and devotion to the local church are increased, but such is actually not the primary end which the right kind of local church has in mind. Rather what it sincerely seeks is primarily the spiritual development of the individual and his building up in the faith.

This purpose lies back of its worship, its Christian education program, and its pastoral ministry. It thinks in terms of children to be taught, young people to be inspired, new Christians to be developed, hearts to be comforted, and minds to be challenged, rather than in terms of its own enhancement as an institution. In an earlier day Methodism used to challenge its ministers in their attempts to serve people to do all in their power "to perfect them in love." This still represents the goal of the local church so far as its own constituency is concerned—"to perfect them in love"—to lead them to love God with all their hearts and their neighbor as themselves and to understand what it really means to love and what it costs.

A local church is in mission when it seeks to add to and does add to the whole number of Christ's disciples. A local church deserving of its name can never be content with the people it is already reaching. It forever remembers that its Master said, "And other sheep I have, which are not of this fold: them also I must bring." It joins him gladly in this task and refusing to be content with the ninety and nine it already has in the fold it goes out to seek diligently even one sheep that is lost.

A local church is in mission when it seeks to transform its immediate community. Its first responsibility is to the neighborhood in the midst of which it is set. This is its Jerusalem where according to the mandate of the Master its ever-widening witness is to begin. The very nature of the church demands that the local church serve the people who live immediately around it. As time moves on and the complexion of the neighborhood changes, so the church must change also. Serving the immediate neighborhood will necessarily require adaptation of the program of the local church in order to meet the needs of its people now living there. Such adaptation of program will necessitate full understanding of what these needs are, the exercise of imagination to know how to respond to them adequately, and the willingness to make available the personnel and monetary resources needed for such program. The local church must guard against any narrow concept of the service it is called upon to render. The total needs of the community are to be kept in mind with a view to total involvement in the total life of the community. Whatever it happens to be that promises to improve the total picture in the community about it is a matter of proper concern for that local church that desires truly to be in mission.

A local church is in mission when it maintains the perspective of a world horizon. The problems are so complex and the demands so numerous in every community that each local church today finds itself facing what is essentially a new temptation. This is the temptation to focus its attention altogether upon its local situation and to devote its energies and resources to improving this. This is understandable especially in the light of increased urbanization, the all too common problem of poverty, and the utter frustration so often felt by youth and by minorities in a day like our own. Such concerns naturally prompt the local church to concentrate near at hand. To a certain extent this is as it should be, but on the other hand no local church can afford to forget that it is also a part of the larger world and that however remote some of the problems of the larger world may appear, they are nevertheless its problems also, for it is necessarily a part of all mankind. It is this that the Master had in mind when he reminded his disciples that they had not only a responsibility in Jerusalem but also "unto the uttermost parts of the earth." It is only the local church which maintains the balance of the far horizon that is truly the local church in mission in the fullest sense of the term.

A local church is in mission when as a totality it is vitally involved in mission. It is not enough for it to have the services and leadership of an able and respected minister. It is not enough for it to possess a skilled and versatile professional staff. Beyond this the entire congregation must be truly involved in mission. This means that all the laymen and laywomen must become full and active participants in the Christian enterprise rather than merely spectators or supporters. It means that at work, at home, and in the community they must translate into action the things that they have learned under the church's instruction and the inspiration they have experienced through the church's worship. It means that young people must be allowed to make their contribution of insight and zeal and dedication. It means that children too have their place in mission, for especially in the kingdom there is much to be learned from the child.

THE CONCEPT OF THE LOCAL CHURCH

Organization for Mission

United Methodism not only has believed and does believe that the local church exists for mission, but it has taken consistently the position that the local church must be organized for mission. Methodists have always majored on organization not for organization's sake, but for the sake of the accomplishment of practical aims. Beginning with the simple original plan for the organizing of each religious society into classes and bands, Methodism has made numerous changes in its provisions for the organization of its local churches as the years have come and gone. Generally the Disciplinary provision for the organization of the local church has become more and more complex, thus presenting a genuine problem particularly for smaller churches. Happily the latest development in legislation for the organization of the local church allows more latitude for the local church to develop its own patterns than did previous legislation. In particular the provision for a local church Council on Ministries, opens the way for each church to face with latitude its total task realistically, effectively, and in the light of its own peculiar local situation.

The administrative body for each local United Methodist Church is the Administrative Board which must meet at least quarterly, but which normally meets monthly in most churches. Its membership is made up, as specified by the *Discipline,* of persons holding certain local church positions plus a number of members-at-large according to the size of the local church. The Administrative Board has general oversight of the administration and program of the local church, receiving reports from the various agencies of the local church and providing for budget needs to implement the various features of the

107

church program. It has a continuing responsibility to cultivate in the local church full participation in Christian mission both locally and far beyond the bounds of the local parish.

Because all its members are automatically members of the Charge Conference which meets at least once a year under the direction of the district superintendent, the Administrative Board has thereby opportunity for continuing contact with connectional United Methodism and for full participation in the ongoing life of the denomination.

Every United Methodist local church must have a Board of Trustees. In cases where several local churches are linked together these may be a Charge Board of Trustees if desired. The number of trustees must be no less than three and no more than nine as may be locally desired. The trustees are empowered to hold and manage the property and other assets of the congregation. They are not independent, but are responsible to the Administrative Board and ultimately to the Charge Conference and can buy, sell, mortgage, remodel or repair property, or undertake new construction only as authorized to do so.

The local church Council on Ministries is a way of getting things accomplished in mission that should be accomplished at the local church level. It is amenable to the Administrative Board to which it is to submit its plans for revision and appropriate action. Its basic membership is made up of the minister and other staff persons; representative of the various work areas—ecumenical affairs, education, evangelism, mission, social concerns, stewardship and worship; coordinators of work with children, young people, adults, and family life; and official representatives of various program agencies of the local church. The Council on Ministries is called upon to exercise creative imagination to carry out its responsibilities through the organizations of the church, through committees to which continuing responsibility is given, and through special task groups created from time to time to meet temporary situations and needs.

The local church remains for United Methodism one of its most important points of decision. Here the elective process of the denomination is basically lodged. Here much of the initiative lies for the recruiting and recommendation of ministerial candidates. Here the right of petition to the General Conference comes to its sharpest and most effective focus. Here through the Pastoral Relations Committee recommendations are made to the bishop relative to the pastoral appointment to the church. And here the decision is made as to the extent to which the local congregation will support the program of and cooperate with the church at large.

The local churches of United Methodism represent thousands of flocks who need a shepherd. They represent millions of persons, old and young, rich and poor, gifted and limited, spiritually mature and spiritually immature, many of whom love the church deeply, and all of whom need the church greatly. They represent also the chief resources of the larger church in both personnel and money. And they represent the basic units through which the larger church must operate to reach people, to create a Christian conscience, and to establish righteousness in the earth.

XI

The Concept of the Annual Conference

No feature of United Methodist Church life is more singular than the concept of the Annual Conference. This is distinctive of United Methodism and is in no small measure one of the secrets of whatever growth and effectiveness in mission it has been able to register.

This most important feature of United Methodist economy came into being originally almost by accident. In 1744, just six years after his conversion and when his evangelistic labors were yet in their beginnings, it occurred to John Wesley that there would be value in calling together a group of kindred spirits for council. The meeting was held at the Foundery in London. Ten persons were present including Wesley and his brother Charles, four lay preachers, and four clergymen of the Church of England. So profitable did this meeting prove that conferences were held by Wesley yearly after that. The strong and effective British Conference which continues to meet annually is the present-day successor to these early conferences.

The first Annual Conference of Methodism in the

United States was held at St. George's Church in Philadelphia in June 1773. Thomas Rankin, one of Wesley's emissaries to America, presided, and there were ten preachers present.

Both Philip Otterbein and Jacob Albright followed the pattern of bringing their fellow laborers together for consultation. The first Annual Conference of the United Brethren Church was held in Frederich County, Maryland, in 1800. The first conference of the Evangelical Association known as the "Original Conference" was held at Kleinfeltersville, Pennsylvania, in 1807 although there was a council of the denomination as early as 1803.

Following 1773 the entire body of Methodist preachers in America was called together in Annual Conference. As the work grew, and because of the difficulty of travel, for a time the custom was followed of having the preachers within a general locality meet together and then in turn those in other localities. These necessarily separate meetings were considered as in effect adjourned sessions of yet one conference. At length in 1796 the total work was divided into six conferences: the Philadelphia, the New England, the Baltimore, the Virginia, the South Carolina, and the Western.

Subsequently Annual Conferences were organized among Methodists from one end of the continent to the other. Normally these conferences were limited in geographic territory because of the difficulties of travel in an earlier day. Often their boundaries were determined by the courses of the rivers which then were the most convenient means of transportation. As the years passed in addition to the geographic Annual Conferences, conferences were organized for racial and ethnic groups including Negroes, Orientals, Germans, Scandinavians, Indians, and Spanish Americans. These conferences all wrote a significant record of service the story of which has largely remained untold and much of which is today largely forgotten. All these racial and ethnic conferences have now been merged with the surrounding geographic conferences except the Indian Mission in Oklahoma and the Rio Grande Conference in the Southwest.

The story of conference development in the Evangelical United Brethren tradition was parallel to that in the Methodist tradition except that no racial or ethnic conferences were established. Because the work of the United Brethren Church and the Evangelical Association was for so long largely among German immigrants and their descendents, the conferences of these churches were over a long period of years largely German-speaking conferences.

In late years due to present-day ease of travel and in the interest of greater efficiency, there has been a trend away from the smaller Annual Conference and many of these former smaller conferences have now been consolidated into larger conferences. Today there are seventy conferences of The United Methodist Church within the United States and thirty-four conferences outside the United States. There are also three missionary conferences—the Alaska, the Oklahoma Indian, and the Red Bird in Appalachia.

Changes in Conference Membership

For long years, in fact for about a century, Annual Conferences in the United States were composed of only traveling preachers. At times they met behind closed doors although normally some public services were held in connection with them. Those were usually in the beginning evangelistic services in which scores of people were converted, and an Annual Conference session without converts would have once been considered a poor session indeed. At length, beginning in 1866 with the Methodist Episcopal Church, South, lay representation in the Annual Conference was provided for. In all the churches except the Methodist Protestant, lay representation in the Annual Conference was at first somewhat limited; but today every charge, no matter how small, is entitled to at least one lay delegate.

Recent years have witnessed a somewhat radical departure from previous practice by provision for ex officio membership in the Annual Conference. This is limited, however, and thus far includes only the conference lay leader, the conference president of United Methodist Women, the conference president of United Methodist Men, and the president of the conference youth organization. The 1970 General Conferences adopted legislation providing for two youth members from each district of the Annual Conference thus insuring that the voice of the younger life of the church shall be heard at this strategic point, even as provision is now made for it to be heard in other councils of United Methodism.

Each United Methodist Annual Conference is a continuing entity. Its ministerial membership changes from year to year as some ministers pass away or transfer to other conferences, and other ministers are admitted into the conference. Its lay membership changes annually as fresh delegates may be elected by the respective Charge Conferences. It is not unusual, however, for the same lay delegates to be sent from year to year and these provide something of a lay continuity, and some of them take obvious lay leadership at the conference level.

A few of the present Annual Conferences have as much as one hundred fifty to one hundred eighty years of unbroken history behind them, the oldest carrying the same name being the Baltimore, the Virginia, and the South Carolina. All the present conferences look back ultimately to those small first conferences meeting in Philadelphia in 1773, in Frederich County, Maryland, in 1800, and in Kleinfeltersville in 1807.

Annual Conference Functioning

Each Annual Conference operates basically through the local churches subject to its appointments and located within its geographic boundaries. It is in these that the life and work of the conference comes to sharpest focus. They represent its chief outlets for the accomplishment of mission and its chief source of supply for the personnel and the financial resources needed for mission. In proportion to the degree that its local churches reach people and help them to grow spiritually, and to the extent that these same churches respond to human need of every kind and everywhere, the Annual Conference of which they are so large a part writes a record of effectiveness or lack of effectiveness in mission.

Each Annual Conference perfects its own organization. Annual Conferences may be incorporated, and many of them are. Most have assets of various kinds such as property and endowment funds held for the conference by its trustees. All conferences have a Council on Ministries, and most have a staff of some size and often a headquarters building. A number of conferences have a paper published bimonthly or monthly to promote the work within the conference. The *Discipline* now leaves each Annual Conference free to develop or not develop structure paralleling the general agency structure of the church as it may see fit.

Each United Methodist conference operates also

through institutions to which it is related as owner, sponsor, or in such other manner as the charter of the institution may determine. These conference-related institutions represent a wide variety of forms of service including schools, colleges, student centers, hospitals, community centers, homes for children, homes for elderly people, and hostels for youth. The late years have seen a rapid proliferation of conference-sponsored institutions or projects representing newer forms of service. Some are designed to minister to the poor whether in the ghetto and pocket areas of the city or in blighted or remote rural areas. Some are beamed at helping persons who have particular needs such as the unemployed, youth who have become dropouts from school, working mothers, or preschool children. Some are set to serve those who are often overlooked and forgotten in our society such as retarded children, released prisoners, or lonely elderly persons. Each Annual Conference has its own interesting story to tell of institutions and projects which in one way or another it supports. The full story of the total institutional service of the Annual Conferences across almost two centuries is one that also has never been told. It can now never be told adequately, for much of it has become lost history, but if it could be told in its entirety it would be an amazing story indeed.

All United Methodist conferences operate further through their connections with the wider church. It is through these connections that they find it possible to carry out the mandate of the Master to be witnesses unto the ends of the earth. Through their gifts to World Service, the Advance, the Ministerial Education Fund, and other important general funds of the church they help to make possible the worldwide ministry of United Methodism. The general agencies of the church with their significant and far-reaching programs of service on both a national and worldwide scale, in effect, represent all the Annual Conferences and make it possible for each of them to render that service beyond its own borders that the Lord of the church called for when he affirmed that the witness was not to stop with Jerusalem and Judea.

The Basic Body

According to the Constitution (Paragraph 37) the Annual Conference is the basic body in United Methodism. It is by the Annual Conference that the ministry of the church is received and elected to orders, reviewed annually as to character and administration, and continued in the effective relationship or retired. It is in the Annual Conference that the ministry is appointed, and it is by the Annual Conference that retirement at length comes.

Likewise it is in the Annual Conference that every charge in the connection has continuing representation through its lay delegate. Here also is lodged its right of petition and appeal.

Furthermore, it is here that the delegates to the General Conference, the law-making body of the church, are elected, and it is here that all actions of the General Conference that are of such moment as to involve constitutional change must be finally ratified by two-thirds vote before they can become effective.

It is thus not the episcopacy, the boards, even the General Conference itself that represents the basic body in United Methodism. It is rather the chain of Annual Conferences which goes back some two hundred years to the time when a single conference embraced what was then the entire church in the case of each of the three original churches now constituting United Methodism.

THE CONCEPT OF THE ANNUAL CONFERENCE

The Annual Conference Session

For United Methodists the Annual Conference session has always been, and continues to be even in this exciting era, an event of interest and significance to which they look forward annually. Much of the life of the local churches centers around it as do also many of the religious concerns of the people.

One of the bishops presides in each Annual Conference session. Each year the Council of Bishops releases what is called a plan of episcopal visitation. This is a schedule of the Annual Conference sessions for the entire church showing place, date, and the bishop who is to preside. Normally today this is the bishop assigned to the area by the Jurisdictional or Central Conference. It may be another bishop, however. For long years the bishops assigned a different bishop to hold each conference session. This was in the interest of assuring an itinerant general superintendency. This plan was abandoned some fifty years ago when the church came to believe that more continuity in Annual Conference administration was the part of wisdom. Frequently today the bishop presiding invites some other bishop to be present at a conference session for preaching or some other service, and thus at least some contact is afforded with the wider episcopacy of the church. The *Discipline* still provides that if no bishop is present the conference shall elect a president from among the elders. This provision dates back to pioneer days when travel was difficult and even hazardous and when the bishop assigned was sometimes delayed in arriving or even altogether unable to reach the seat of the conference. This remains an emergency provision that is seldom used today.

Each Annual Conference elects a secretary for the

quadrennium who becomes responsible for keeping the records of its actions and a treasurer who receives and distributes its funds. Also it elects such annual, standing, and special committees as it may deem necessary for the proper conducting of its business.

Likewise each Annual Conference adopts its own standing rules which may be amended at any conference session by whatever procedure for amendment is outlined in them.

The Annual Conference session represents an occasion for reviewing the work and receiving a report from all the churches. The first Methodist Conference in 1773 asked, "What members are there in the society?" and Annual Conferences have received statistical reports ever since. The reports from the charges are now given by way of a form filled out by each pastor annually. These reports are assembled by the conference statistician and, from them, the annual report of the conference as a whole is compiled. The report of each Annual Conference is forwarded to the General Council on Finance and Administration which gathers all the Annual Conference reports and compiles a report for the entire connection. This report is published in a volume called the General Minutes.

The Annual Conference session is also an occasion for planning, particularly for planning the program of the conference for the coming year. The proposed program is worked out by the Conference Council on Ministries and its related agencies and submitted to the conference for amendment, rejection, or adoption. In most conferences today the proposed program is embodied in a booklet which is placed in the hands of all delegates and ministers approximately thirty days ahead of the conference session so that there may be ample time for all to reflect upon it carefully and be ready with any admendments or substitutions which they may desire to propose.

The Annual Conference session is likewise a meeting for business. There is much routine business to be attended to in every session including such matters as receiving, dismissing, and retiring ministers; considering various conference causes; taking necessary action regarding conference institutions; caring for conference property matters; setting pension rates; approving budgets; electing trustees; and caring for other numerous administrative details. It is the responsibility of the bishop presiding to see that each item of business which the conference needs to consider receives due attention before it finally adjourns. The age-old Methodist provision for being sure that all necessary conference business is cared for is by way of the method of questions. This method was inaugurated by Wesley; he would propose pertinent questions and seek the answer of the conference. Across the years this method has continued to be followed. Sets of pertinent questions are still placed by the general church in the hands of the bishop presiding, and the receiving of the answers to these questions automatically results in the completion of the primary business of each conference session. Until recently these questions were published in the *Discipline* itself, but as of the last four or six years they have been printed in leaflet form for distribution among the conferences. The final report of each Annual Conference to the general statistical office of the church must be made on these forms.

So far as the bishop presiding is concerned, the Annual Conference session represents his major point of contact with his preachers and his people. They are not his in the sense of possessiveness, but rather they are his in the sense that they are the persons he has been appointed to serve and whom he carries in his heart with abiding love. Here is his golden opportunity to have them together, to preach to them, to challenge them, to encourage them, to dream with them, and to share with them his heart and soul. What any Annual Conference session finally proves to be will depend very largely upon the man who occupies the chair of the conference.

The Annual Conference session is also a time for the ordination of ministers. Frequently in the past the ordination service has represented the high hour of the entire session. It is the bishop who ordains, but it is the conference which elects to deacons and elders orders. Back of this election lies a long period of training in college and seminary for the fledgling minister and an involved and careful sifting process upon the part of the Conference Board of the Ministry before making its recommendation to the conference regarding the candidate. Heretofore the ordination of all ministers except in extreme emergencies has come at the Annual Conference session. The reasoning back of this custom is the fact that ordination in United Methodist thinking is a conference function rather than a local church function and the further desirability of affording the rich memories that the members of a class can carry across the years of having been ordained together. In more recent years some bishops have sometimes followed the pattern of ordaining men in the local churches from which they come. There is nothing in the *Discipline* to forbid this, for once a man is elected to orders by an Annual Conference any United Methodist bishop is at liberty to ordain him anywhere, any time. The record of such ordinations in local churches, however, must be entered into the official records of the succeeding Annual Conference.

The Annual Conference session is unique in United

Methodism in that it is the time for the deployment or re-deployment of the ministry. The last question on the agenda of the conference session is the quaint historic question, "Where are the preachers stationed this year?" Most Annual Conference sessions close with the reading of the appointments, although generally today they are all known long before they are read. There was a time even within the memory of many persons still in middle life when such was not the case. In many conferences, and under the exercise of the appointing power upon the part of of many bishops, preachers did not know where they were going until the appointments were actually read, and churches did not know what minister they were to have for the ensuing year. There was something dramatic and deeply moving about it—a body of men waiting silently for their marching orders and then proceeding to their appointments not always gladly or even willingly, but nevertheless loyally in a day when almost no Methodist or Evangelical United Brethren preacher would want to be thought of as rejecting his appointment and refusing to go where he was sent. In the growing democratic atmosphere of our own day much of this has changed. There is now consultation with both minister and church, and the surprise element in the reading of the appointments has gone. Nevertheless, the final decision in the appointments is still left ultimately with the appointing power, and a high proportion of ministers having been given some opportunity to express themselves are still content to leave it there. The same is true of most United Methodist churches. They do ask for the privilege of expressing their choices, but in the end they normally accept in good spirit the appointment worked out by the bishop and the cabinet.

An Annual Conference session should be, and can be, a spiritual experience for all those in attendance. This has been the accepted ideal from the beginning, though the ideal has not always been realized. The conference session should be a time of great preaching, great dreaming, great planning, and great undertaking. It should prove a tonic for the soul and a time of inspiration that will send preachers and lay people back to their churches with new courage, new determination, new vision, and with a fresh call to ministry.

Annual Conference sessions are undergoing change today just as is everything else in life. They are a far cry from the Annual Conference sessions of even half a century ago when life was lived largely in isolation and when the preachers saw each other only at conference time. Then the traditional hymn for the opening of conference, "And are we yet alive, and see each other's face?" had particular and moving pertinence. Today isolation has been overcome, distance has been bridged, and preachers and lay persons see each other with frequency. Moreover, some of the experiences that once lent color to conference time are now no more, such as going to conference on the train, being entertained in the homes of the people, and the inevitable mystery and drama that surrounded the final reading of the appointments.

Nevertheless, for United Methodists the Annual Conference session still has its strange magnetic drawing power, and for them basically it is still something of the same fellowship experience and demonstration of the common life of the connection that it has been from the beginning.

XII

The Concept of the General Conference

The General Conference in United Methodism is a striking example of the tendency of the church from the beginning to adjust structure to mission. It developed originally as a matter of practical necessity and so continues unto the present hour. No New Testament precedent is claimed for it as a form of church polity, and no appeal is made to the history of the church across the ages in its defense. It is nothing more and nothing less than simply a device to meet the continuing situation in United Methodist Church life.

The Delegated General Conference

In the earliest days the Methodist work in the United States was small and marked by a minimum of organization. All the preachers serving the Methodist societies met together in conference once a year.

Beginning in 1792 the church met in General Conference once every four years. All the preachers of the church in full connection were members of this body. It had at that time no lay membership. The first five General Conferences were held in Baltimore and the sixth in New York. As the work expanded southward, northward, and westward, it became increasingly difficult for all the preachers to attend due to the great difficulties of travel at that time. This meant that a higher proportion of the preachers living nearer the chosen site of the General Conference could be present while a much lower proportion could be present of those living farther away.

It was out of the need to meet this practical situation that in the General Conference of 1808 the proposal was approved for a delegated General Conference, the delegates to be chosen by the respective Annual Conferences according to a prescribed formula. This proposal was approved by the Annual Conferences, and the first delegated General Conference to assemble was that of 1812.

The wisdom of having a delegated General Conference as a practical working arrangement for a connectional church has been verified by more than a century and a half of church experience. The plan continues to work effectively for a connection now involving more than eleven million members and scattered over much of the globe.

The United Brethren Church and the Evangelical Association followed much of the same pattern of development and for the same reasons. The first General Conference of the United Brethren Church was that of 1815 and the first of the Evangelical Association was that of 1816.

When the idea of a delegated General Conference was born a four-year cycle seemed reasonable enough, for life in that day moved at a leisurely pace. For long years this schedule of meeting went unchallenged. In more recent years as the tempo of life has become greatly accelerated and changes have come so swiftly, there have been those who have questioned whether a quadrennial meeting of the General Conference is sufficient. The 1972 General Conference adopted, therefore, an amendment providing that the General Conference must meet every four years, but may by its own order meet every two years, but no more frequently than this. This amendment was rejected, however, in the voting in the Annual Conferences. Under the law, however, a special session of the General Conference may be called by the Council of Bishops if necessary or may be ordered by the previous General Conference.

A Representative Body

The General Conference as a delegated body is representative of the entire church. All the Annual Conferences are represented. Delegates are elected upon a two-factor basis: (1) the number of ministerial members of the Annual Conference, and (2) the number of church members in the Annual Conference. The clerical members are elected by the clerical members of the Annual Conferences and the lay members by the lay members of the Annual Conferences who have themselves in turn been elected by the members of the various Charge Conferences. There is only elected membership in the General Conference. In recent years the General Conference has seen fit to seat certain youth representatives in an effort to afford involvement by the youth of the church, but this seating has been with voice but without vote. Fraternal delegates from related autonomous churches are also seated with voice but without vote. The general secretaries of the church have the privilege of voice but not vote when matters related to their particular agencies are under discussion. The bishops of the church are not members of the General Conference and are accorded neither voice nor vote. The same holds for members of the Judicial Council.

Responsibilities of the General Conference

The General Conference is not only a delegated representative body. It is also a body given clearly designated responsibilities. The includes the authority to legislate on all matters purely connectional, including such matters as church membership, the ministry, Annual, Jurisdictional, Central, and General Conference organization, local church organization, church property, church fiscal policy, the judicial system of the church, and the general board and agency organization of the church. It also has authority to conduct certain elections, chiefly that of members of the Judicial Council.

A quorum is necessary for the General Conference to do business. On one occasion at least a General Conference was forced to final adjournment with its business incomplete because of lack of a quorum. This was at St. Louis in 1970.

While the General Conference is a body to which great responsibility is delegated, this designation of power is not without limitation. The fathers in Methodism in setting up in 1808 the provision for a delegated General Conference established what they termed the Restrictive Rules. These rules provided that there were certain matters upon which the General Conference could not act with finality. Its action in these matters would have to be confirmed in the subsequent Annual Conference sessions by a two-thirds and in some cases three-fourths vote of the Annual Conference members present and voting.

These Methodist Restrictive Rules were taken over into The United Methodist Church and a seventh rule was added, granting to the former membership of the Evangelical United Brethren Church certain guarantees during the early years of union.

The seven Restrictive Rules provide that the General Conference shall not take the following actions without a confirming vote of the membership of the Annual Conferences.

1. It shall not change the Articles of Religion or establish new standards or rules of doctrine contrary to our present existing standards of doctrine.
2. It shall not revoke, alter, or change our Confession of Faith.
3. It shall not do away with episcopacy or destroy the plan of an itinerant general superintendency.
4. It shall not do away with the right of trial or appeal.
5. It shall not revoke or change the General Rules.
6. It shall not appropriate the net income of the publishing houses to other than the benefit of retired ministers, their wives, widows, and children.
7. It shall not do away with proper and effective representation for the former Evangelical United Brethren Church at all conference levels and in all agencies or the twelve years following union in 1968. In 1980 this rule will automatically be deleted from the Constitution.

The first portion of the *Discipline* contains what is known as the Constitution of the church. The Constitution represents a clear delineation of the basic structure of the church. This part of the *Discipline* cannot be changed except by a majority vote of the General Conference followed by approval of two-thirds of the members of all the Annual Conferences present and voting. The Evangelical United Brethren Church had a similar provision for a constitutional section of their *Discipline*. All other parts of the United Methodist *Discipline* may be changed by any General Conference by simple majority vote.

Subject to Judicial Interpretation

All legislation passed by the General Conference is subject to interpretation by the Judicial Council as to its constitutionality or its actual meaning. Interpretation of the constitutionality of legislation or proposed legislation can be made by the Judicial Council only upon appeal by the Council of Bishops or by the General Conference itself. The Judicial Council may review the legality of actions taken by various church bodies or render a declaratory decision on the meaning of legislation upon request of a College of Bishops, an Annual Conference, a Jurisdictional or Central Conference, or certain boards and agencies of the church.

The Judicial Council also reviews the decisions of law made in the Annual Conferences by the bishops.

Speaking for and to the Church

The General Conference is a delegated body speaking for and to the church. From the beginning it has been customary for it to pass resolutions on what have been regarded as pertinent subjects for its consideration and has addressed communications to the general church.

In late years it has spoken increasingly on a wide range of matters related to the general welfare, not only of the church itself, but likewise of society as a whole. The resolutions thus adopted represent the majority opinion of those present and voting. As such they then represent the official position of The United Methodist Church on a particular matter at that particular time. Only the General Conference may speak officially for the church. Resolutions adopted by a General Conference may be altered by succeeding General Conferences or reversed or supplanted as changes appear in the thinking of delegates. Whatever binding effect they ultimately prove to have in the life of the church and the thinking of its membership must adhere finally in the actual validity of the argument they present.

The resolutions on miscellaneous subjects approved by each succeeding General Conference are embodied in a *Book of Resolutions* and thus released to the church for study and action. The Board of Church and Society and the Board of Discipleship in particular have responsibility for keeping these judgments of the General Conference before the attention of the church and interpreting them as may prove necessary.

Working Procedures

The General Conference is a deliberative and legislative body which operates through clearly defined working procedures.

All members of the General Conference are involved in these working procedures. There are fourteen legislative committees, and each member of the General Conference is assigned to one of these committees. The legislative committees are as follows:

1. Christian Social Concerns
2. Conferences
3. Education

4. Lay Activities and Church Finance
5. Membership and Evangelism
6. Clergy
7. Missions
8. Pensions
9. Communications and Publications
10. Health and Welfare
11. Ecumenical Concerns
12. Judicial Administration
13. Local Church
14. Rituals and Orders of Worship

All members of the General Conference make their own committee selection in their Annual Conference delegation.

In addition to the legislative committees there are also eleven administrative committees designed to expedite the business of the General Conference. These administrative committees are smaller and do not include all members of the General Conference. They are as follows:

1. Committee on Agenda
2. Committee on Presentation of Reports
3. Committee on Correlation and Editorial Revision
4. Committee on Courtesies and Privileges
5. Committee on Credentials
6. Committee on Fraternal Delegates
7. Committee on Journal
8. Committee on Plan of Organization and Rules of Order
9. Committee on Presiding Officers
10. Committee on Reference
11. Committee of Tellers

The members of the administrative committees are nominated by the Council of Bishops.

The legislative committees meet for long hours, particularly in the early days of the General Conference. Each legislative committee submits its work to the General Conference by way of a series of reports, each report dealing with only a single legislative item. Such report may propose the addition of a new paragraph to the *Discipline,* the deletion of a previous one, or the alteration of a previous one. Each committee report must include a record of the number of committee members voting for or against the proposed report and the number of members abstaining. If as many as ten members or one-tenth of the membership of a committee are opposed to the report as approved by the majority, they may submit a minority report which then has the same right of consideration by the General Conference as does the majority report.

Of particular interest to all United Methodists is the manner in which the respective legislative committees of the General Conference receive their working material. The petitions received from throughout the church by the secretary of the General Conference are allocated by the Committee on Reference to the appropriate legislative committee for consideration. Every petition thus received must be considered by the committee to which it is assigned. The committee has the option of reporting to the General Conference a recommendation of either concurrence or of nonconcurrence, but it must report some recommendation. If the committee is minded to recommend concurrence with the substance of a petition, it has the power to amend or modify the petition as originally presented as may appear wise to it.

The General Conference meets in plenary session, usually at least once each day. As the legislative committees complete their work and the conference moves toward adjournment, plenary sessions are normally held three times daily. The opening plenary session is usually given over to a service of holy communion. Then follows a period given to the organization of the conference and a session devoted to hearing the Episcopal Address. The Episcopal Address normally contains numerous recommendations which, by formal motion, are usually referred to the appropriate committees for consideration and report to the conference.

Other plenary sessions are devoted in whole or in part to receiving fraternal messengers, hearing certain persons present particular causes and programs, and the witnessing of certain presentations usually of a dramatic and inspirational nature. Each morning plenary session opens with a period of worship conducted by one of the bishops chosen by the Council of Bishops.

The greater part of the plenary sessions of the General Conference is given to considering the reports of the various legislative committees. There are literally hundreds of these. Generally only the reports in which concurrence is recommended are considered, although a procedure is provided by which a report on which nonconcurrence is recommended may be lifted up for the consideration of the General Conference.

For the expediting of its work as it moves through its total business, the General Conference adopts at its organizing session a set of Rules of Order. These are spelled out in detail and printed in a handbook for delegates. They make possible the smooth operation of what would otherwise be an almost unwieldy body with an almost impossible agenda as they set forth the parliamentary procedures to be observed.

A most interesting feature of every General Conference is the *Daily Christian Advocate* which is placed upon the desk of each delegate each morning. A binder is provided for the daily copies so that by the time the conference reaches its late days the delegate has in his possession a volume of considerable size. All reports to be considered by the General Conference must be printed in the *Daily Christian Advocate,* and they cannot be considered until they have been before the delegates in this way for at least twenty-four hours except by suspension of the rules. The *Daily Christian Advocate* also contains a verbatim report of the previous day's proceedings. This working volume is used by every delegate almost every minute of every plenary session where legislative matters are under consideration.

Indispensable to the operation of any General Conference is the secretarial staff. The key person in the secretarial staff is the secretary of the General Conference who is elected quadrennially and who need not be a member of the body. The secretary elected nominates a number of assistants to whom are delegated various segments of the total secretarial responsibility. The secretary of the General Conference may be a minister or a lay person as the General Conference may choose.

The role of the bishops in the General Conference is a somewhat limited one, and whatever weight they may carry there is the weight of whatever personal influence any one of them or all of them collectively may have rather than any growing out of some prerogatives of office. The bishops cannot vote, and they do not speak except by request of the General Conference. Their one, time-honored opportunity to have their voice heard is through the Episcopal Address. The bishops are the presiding officers of the General Conference and the selection of the bishop to occupy the chair at a particular session is made and announced by the Committee on Presiding Officers which is made up of lay and clerical delegates. Up until now the bishops as a body are seated upon the platform, and the same seating arrangement obtains for members of the Judicial Council. They also do not speak, and they cannot be members of the General Conference. Periodically throughout the General Conference as may be necessary, the Judicial Council announces its decisions on matters properly referred to it.

The actions of a General Conference become effective with its adjournment unless otherwise ordered.

Writing a Discipline

The final product of each session of a General Conference is a new *Discipline* for The United Methodist Church. The *Discipline* is edited by the book editor of the church, assisted by a Committee of Correlation appointed by the General Conference and by the secretary of the General Conference. The new issue embodies all the deletions from and additions to the previous *Discipline* brought about by the legislative actions of the General Conference. In addition, as has been previously stated, the various resolutions adopted by the General Conference are embodied by the book editor in *The Book of Resolutions* which is also published quadrennially.

XIII

The Concept of Jurisdictions

The jurisdictional system in United Methodism dates back to the union of the Methodist Episcopal Church, the Methodist Episcopal Church, South, and the Methodist Protestant Church in 1939. It was carried over into The United Methodist Church in 1968. Originally there were six jurisdictions within the United States, five of them geographic and one, the Central Jurisdiction, composed of the Negro Annual Conferences. Today the Central Jurisdiction has been eliminated, and there are now five geographic jurisdictions, the Northeastern, Southeastern, North Central, South Central, and Western.

After some forty long years of union negotiations between the three Methodist churches and the rejection of several different plans of union, the key to union finally appeared in the proposal for jurisdictions. In recent years it has been affirmed by some that it was the provision for setting aside the Negro Conferences in a separate jurisdiction that made Methodist union possible. It must be admitted that there is some truth in this statement, so far as some persons in the South who were voting on union in 1939 were concerned. But such is not the full truth. Totally aside from the provision for the Central Jurisdiction it is seriously to be doubted that Methodist union would ever have been voted in 1939 without provision for geographic jurisdictions. It is further to be doubted that the church now could muster the constitutional vote necessary to do away with the jurisdictions, for they represent in the thinking of large numbers of people a constitutional guarantee of diversity within unity. The truth is that every plan of union considered seriously by the three Methodist churches in the course of their forty-year negotiations contained in each case what was in essence at least a jurisdictional provision. The plan of union, for instance, considered in 1924 but rejected provided for all the work composing the Methodist Episcopal Church wherever located to be one jurisdiction and that composing the Methodist Episcopal Church, South, another.

The concept of the jurisdictional system in United Methodism cannot be fully appreciated without at least some passing knowledge of the history that lies behind its establishment.

.In his last letter to America addressed to Ezekial Cooper under date of February 1, 1791, John Wesley wrote, "Lose no opportunity of declaring to all men that the Methodists are one people in all the world."

This was the founder's dream; but the truth of the matter is that Methodists have always experienced some difficulty in being and remaining one people. Historically they have divided a number of times. Sometimes it has been over matters of polity, sometimes over difference of opinion concerning pressing social issues, and sometimes merely for purposes of convenience in the operational life of the church as in the case of the establishment of the autonomous churches. This tendency to divide has been strong enough that despite the unions that have been consumated in England, the United States, and elsewhere, there are still some fifty bodies which bear the name of Methodist and trace their spiritual ancestry to the same spiritual father.

Again, as over against these actual divisions, there have been numerous occasions in both General Conferences and in the general life of the church when division of opinion has become so strong as at least to threaten disruption, and only strong and skilled leadership and the exercise of patience and understanding have been able to prevent such happening.

Perhaps some tendency to divide is to be expected in a church like United Methodism. It has gone everywhere preaching the gospel. It has refused to confine its efforts to any one section of the country, or of the world for that matter. It has sought to address its appeal to all classes and conditions of men. Because it has gone everywhere and has had some measure of success in reaching all kinds of people, there are therefore to be found within its membership all manner of cultural attachments and conflicting loyalties and strong differences of thinking.

On the other hand, just as there has been in Methodism a tendency to divide, so also there has been a tendency to unite, to coalesce, and to stay together which has manifested itself countless times. Basic to the explanation of this tendency to stay together is our common spiritual heritage and our common commitment to the one Lord who said, "one is your Master, even Christ; and all ye are brethren."

When one studies Methodist history carefully one discovers that the proponents of every plan of Methodist union, both those that have failed and those which have succeeded, sought to face realistically these two tendencies. Whatever organizational structure they proposed always represented a concerted effort to suggest a plan of organization which kept in mind these two divergent tendencies and sought to achieve some measure of balance between them.

The jurisdictional system is basically an attempt to reconcile these divergent tendencies. There are solid arguments for its being a basic part of United Methodist strucure.

Structural Recognition of Difference

Doubtless the chief advantage of and strongest argument for the jurisdictional system is the structural recognition which it affords that Methodists living in different localies face differing local situations and are themselves quite different in many ways. These differences are not always major, but they do have significance. Local Methodists can no more divorce themselves from the context in which their day-by-day lives are lived than can other people. New England is not south Georgia, and New York City is considerably different from the Ozark country in Arkansas and Missouri. All of us are more or less affected by the problems, the mores, the ways of thinking, the traditions, and the patterns of life in that part of the world that is called home. For either liberal or conservative to deny this is to fail to be objective. These factors should not, however, be finally determinative but to acknowledge their existence is only to be realistic. This the jurisdictional system does. In so doing, it does something of what the federal system does as it acknowledges the several states as different units, but nevertheless units of a total whole.

Moreover, United Methodists are not only different in the local traditions which are a part of their lives, but to some extent they also differ in their thinking, emphases, and evaluations. In some parts of United Methodism they tend to be more liberal and in others more conservative; in some Methodists come quite close to high churchmanship, while in others they are informal to a fault. Such differences, while often following a general regional pattern, do not always do so. Annual Conferences which lie side by side will differ radically in thinking and practice. It is somewhat suprising to many people to discover that some of the more conservative conferences theologically are to be found in what is generally regarded as the more liberal section of the church—while some quite liberal conferences are found in sections regarded as more conservative.

The jurisdictional system in affording structural recognition of the fact of difference may conceivably therefore serve a laudable end when it is not abused. The church as a whole has opportunity thereby to deal with diversity at a local level and still achieve unity in diversity at the general church level.

The fact is frequently overlooked that the Central Conference system is essentially the jurisdictional system under another name with the exception that some necessary adaptation of the *Discipline* is authorized for the Central Conference that is not authorized for the Jursidictional Conferences. The Central Conference system, like the jurisdictional system is simply a structural recognition that the situation in which United Methodists everywhere find themselves does have local aspects which should not be finally determinative, but which sound wisdom would counsel against overlooking.

Protection of All Parts of the Church

Again the jurisdictional system may be looked upon as protection. It was probably this above all else that was in the minds of those who formulated the 1939 Plan of Union when they incorporated into it the jurisdictional feature. In a church the size of Methodism every part of the church is of necessarily only a minor fraction of the whole. The Southeastern Jurisdictional, with almost three million members, is larger numerically than all but five of the major denominations listed in *The Yearbook of American Churches*. Yet in Methodism, it is a numerical minority. The same holds true for the North Central Jurisdiction with better than two and one-half million members, and the South Central with two million, and the Northeastern with better than two million.

The genius of the jurisdictional system is its protection against any geographical part of the church becoming lost in the bigness of the whole.

It provides this first of all by distributing among the jurisdictions representation upon the various boards and agencies of the church, and allowing the Jurisdictional Conferences to elect such representatives, in the case of most of the general church agencies.

The jurisdictional system provides protection for all geographic minorities also by providing for the election of bishops in the respective Jurisdictional Conferences. There are strong arguments which can be made against this, of course, but whatever may be said of the present episcopacy, it is indeed an episcopacy which in its composition does represent every part of the church. It is somewhat enlightening to consider how geographic minority groups have fared in the election of church leadership when such built-in protection was not provided for. In the ninety-five years between the division of The Methodist Church in 1844 and Methodist union in 1939, the Methodist Episcopal Church had conferences all over the South, yet in all these years, with the exception of several of the black bishops, only one man was ever elected from a Southern conference. In the same period the Methodist Episcopal Church, South, had small conferences in the far West and in some of the north central states, but in this same period in the Methodist Episcopal Church, South, again only one man was ever elected from these conferences. Whether the jurisdictional system results in the election of an episcopacy as widely known in the church at large as might be wished may well be open to question. The fact is not open to question, however, that it does result in a better distributed episcopacy geographically and one in better position to be knowledgeable of the church at all its local levels.

It should be pointed out that under our present law only a jurisdiction has guarantees of representation both on the general boards and in the episcopacy of the church. It does not, however, have guarantee of representation upon the Judicial Council. Annual Conferences have no guarantee of representation anywhere except in the General Conference and in the General Council on Ministries.

A Working Arrangement

The jurisdictional system may also well be considered from the viewpoint of a possible practical working arrangement. Under the jurisdictional system a group of conferences finding themselves with the same general concerns and in contiguous territory may be associated for administrative purposes. This arrangement need not interfere with or destroy the area system. It is simply a natural and convenient grouping of areas and conferences which have some things more or less in common. In some sections of the church in the years since Methodist union in 1939 little has been made of the jurisdictional systems. Whether programwise it might actually make any contribution in these particular sections is not known as it has not been tried. On the other hand, in the Southeastern Jurisdiction and the South Central Jurisdiction serious attempt has been made to take full advantage of the jurisdictional system as a working arrangement.

In the Southeastern Jurisdiction an office has been set up with a staff and working groups organized to deal with such matters as missions, evangelism, social concerns, education, lay work, ecumenical relations, town and country work, and communications. Programs have been developed in these fields and have been promoted through the jurisdiction.

The Southeastern Jurisdiction also gives strong backing to the three seminaries within its bounds—Emory, Gammon, and Duke—and to its Assembly at Lake Junaluska. The custom followed by the assembly of bringing religious leaders from all over the world to its platform has provided for cross-fertilization of thinking which has infinitely enriched the life of the church in the Southeast for now half a century.

The program developed in the South Central Jurisdiction, while not quite so formidable as that in the Southeastern Jurisdiction, has nevertheless been of considerable magnitude and influence.

Possible Disadvantages

While the jurisdictional system has its possible advantages, honesty compels the admission that it may conceivably have its disadvantages also.

THE CONCEPT OF JURISDICTIONS

Undoubtedly, the jurisdictional system may represent a disadvantage when it is little more than something of an expensive formality and when little continuing use is made of it. When it represents no more than a quadrennial Jurisdictional Conference where bishops are elected and nominations made for boards and agencies, it is quite understandable that there are those who should feel that it is entirely too expensive. And, this would appear all the more true at those times when no bishops are due to be elected and when Jurisdictional Conference program committees are forced to look in all directions to find something to occupy the time and attention and energies of the delegates.

Since 1939 three of the jurisdictions have chosen to make little use of the jurisdictional system. There are, of course, reasons for this. One is the general lack of enthusiasm for the jurisdictional system which has characterized these parts of the church from the time of Methodist union. The thinking in these sections has long been a type of thinking which, particularly since the General Conference of 1848 of the Methodist Episcopal Church, has not hesitated to concentrate power in the General Conference. These sections in 1939, however, in the interest of union, graciously took due account of the fear of an all-powerful General Conference obtaining then in the other sections of the uniting church and went along with the checks and balances afforded by the jurisdictional system.

Another often overlooked reason for making little use of the jurisdictional system in three of the jurisdictions is the fact that this section of the church at the time of Methodist union already had the area system; and it was working well. The episcopal areas at the time of union were sufficiently large to afford momentum for the development of and carrying out of an efficient ongoing program, and it is easy to understand why it should be concluded that nothing further organizationally was needed. Since 1939 the number of episcopal areas in the church has increased by fourteen, or almost fifty percent, and the trend promises to continue in this direction. Twenty-one episcopal areas are now comprised of only a single conference and often represent a quite limited geographic area. It may well be that with the current reduction in size of episcopal areas greater momentum for program may need to be achieved upon some broader basis such as that afforded by a jurisdiction.

Another reason for the lack of enthusiasm for the jurisdictional system in some parts of the church has been the absence of institutions jointly owned or operated by all the Annual Conferences of the jurisdiction. Institutions tend to become rallying centers in church life and as such, morale builders. This is true in the case of the majority of Annual Conferences. And it may be true for a jurisdiction also. It should be remembered that part of the secret of the closeness of the conferences of the Southeastern and South Central jurisdictions is accounted for by their historic jurisdictional institutions such as Emory, Southern Methodist University, Lake Junaluska, and Mt. Sequoyah. There is a long history back of this situation, centering particularly about the loss of Vanderbilt University. When Vanderbilt was lost to the church, the Church, South, countered by establishing new institutions more closely related to the General Conference. This broadly based institutional attachment continues in both the Southeastern and South Central jurisdictions and the life of the church in the Southeast and Southwest still centers largely around these jurisdictional institutions. In sections of the church whose history has been otherwise, it is understandable that the institutional argument for the jurisdictional system should not carry too much weight.

It must be acknowledged that conceivably the jurisdictional system may be abused. It will be abused if it is allowed to foster ingrowth of thought or failure to share fully in the efforts of the total church to meet the demands of a new day in the life of the world. It will be abused if in any way it is allowed to contribute to the fragmentation of the church and to move in the direction of a church within a church. What our fathers envisioned in setting up the jurisdictional system was certainly not brokenness, but merely provision for a reasonable degree of diversity within genuine unity.

With both its possible advantages and its possible handicaps, we shall probably have the jurisdictional system with us for some time to come. Wisdom would seem to dictate that, this being the case, more genuinely creative thinking should still be done as to ways and means to make the jurisdictional system contribute more effectively to the total life of the total church.

The Jurisdictional Conference

The jurisdictional system comes to focus in the Jurisdictional Conference which meets every four years following the regular General Conference session. Under the law all Jurisdictional conferences must meet at the same time. The purpose of this is primarily to facilitate the transfer of bishops from one jurisdiction to another should such prove desirable.

The Jurisdictional Conference is composed of an equal number of clerical and lay delegates elected by the Annual Conferences. The delegates to the General Conference are also the first delegates to the Jurisdictional Conference.

To these is added a number of additional delegates from each conference sufficient to bring the delegation up to the quota of Jurisdictional Conference delegates to which the Annual Conference is entitled.

The Jurisdictional Conference meets usually for about five days. It includes business sessions and sessions devoted to special presentations and observances. The active bishops of the jurisdiction preside in turn. As in the General Conference all delegates are assigned to committees.

The Jurisdictional Conference reviews the work of the previous quadrennium and plans any desired jurisdictional program for the quadrennium ahead. It reviews the character and administration of the bishops. It establishes the episcopal residences and assigns the active bishops to them. It retires bishops and elects new ones. It elects representatives to various general and jurisdictional agencies. It fixes the geographic boundaries of the Annual Conferences of the jurisdiction. It also gives implementation to the program of the general church at the jurisdictional level.

XIV

The Concept of the Central Conference

As early as 1833 the Methodist Episcopal Church began work in Liberia, and as early as 1847 and 1848 the Methodist Episcopal Church and the Methodist Episcopal Church, South, began work in China. Overseas work began in the Evangelical Association in 1851 in Germany and in 1854 in Africa. The United Brethren Church began work in Puerto Rico in 1899 and in the Philippines in 1901. The eighteen hundreds were the golden era of missionary expansion, and the churches now forming United Methodism fell into step with what was happening throughout the then Christian world. Missionaries were sent out, converts were made, and congregations were organized. The movement spread rapidly until by the time the period of missionary expansion had reached its climax, United Methodism was working with enthusiasm in about half a hundred nations scattered over the world. The Methodist Episcopal Church in particular was commonly spoken of and thought of as "a world church."

As the work overseas developed in the three Methodist

churches and likewise in the Evangelical and United Brethren churches, Annual Conferences were organized having the same prerogatives and privileges as all other Annual Conferences of the church.

Earlier Patterns of Administration

The question soon arose as to how these churches and conferences were to be administered by the episcopacy of the church. The plan first followed and continued over a long period of time was for them to be included in the annual plan of episcopal visitation just as were all other conferences of the church. Some bishop, often a different bishop, was sent out from the homeland each year to hold the Annual Conferences in other lands.

The theory back of this arrangement was the traditional Methodist position that the episcopacy is a general superintendency and that all the bishops are bishops of all the church. From a practical viewpoint, however, this plan did not allow for continuity of leadership, and the annual coming of some bishop to visit the work and hold the Annual Conference session became largely only symbolic.

Beginning late in the last century the Methodist Episcopal Church developed what was termed the "missionary episcopacy." According to this plan the General Conference would elect a bishop for a specific missionary field, and his episcopal authority would be limited to this particular field. At first there was resistance to this plan because both in theory and practice it collided with the important Methodist concept of a fully general superintendency. Nevertheless, in time it found acceptance, and for a period it made significant contribution to the life of the church. The story of the missionary episcopacy in Methodism has not been adequately told. It is a fascinating story indeed and includes some of the unforgettable characters of Methodist history such as William Taylor elected bishop for Africa in 1884, James M. Thoburn whose tracks are yet to be seen in India and Southeast Asia, J. C. Hartzell of Africa, F. W. Warne of India, and others. The last of the line of missionary bishops were Edwin F. Lee of the Philippines who died in 1948 and John M. Springer of Africa who died in 1963. The *Discipline* still contains a definition of a missionary bishop, but this legislation is largely a dead letter. It appears that the missionary bishop has now definitely passed in the life of the world and the church.

The Methodist Episcopal Church, South, and the United Brethren Church had no missionary bishops, and the Methodist Protestant Church had no bishops at all. The Evangelical Association had a missionary bishop at one period.

The earlier years of the present century saw the development in the Methodist Episcopal Church of the area system with each bishop assigned for a quadrennium to a particular residence and to continuing administration of a particular area. In due time episcopal residences were established overseas in India, Singapore, Manila, China, Japan, Korea, Latin America, and Europe, and bishops were assigned to such residences just as in the United States. This plan had its distinct advantages in that it provided for on-the-field residence, but it also had its disadvantages insofar as it usually meant non-native episcopal leadership, and what was more serious, was subject to too constant turnover. Many bishops upon being elected to office were first assigned to some overseas residence, but after only one quadrennium often found their way to assignment to some residence in the United States. The story of this period of episcopal residence on the field has likewise not been told adequately, and it deserves telling. It covers the services of some of the great episcopal figures of Methodist history such as James W. Bashford in China, Herbert Welch in Korea, John L. Nuelson in Europe, George A. Miller in Latin America, and Benton T. Bradley in India. It also includes some of the most heroic chapters in the long story of the expansion of the church.

The Central Conference

In 1928 the Methodist Episcopal Church moved to what is now known as the Central Conference pattern. Under this pattern the work within a given geographical area is organized into what is known as a Central Conference. A Central Conference is similar in general to a Jurisdictional Conference in the United States with the important exception that the Jurisdictional Conference has no power to develop a supplemental *Discipline* of its own. A Central Conference has the power to edit and publish a Central Conference *Discipline* under certain limitations. It also has power to make certain adaptations of the legislation of the *Discipline* regarding the local church, the ministry, advices, worship, and temporal economy. Back of this grant of power lies the realization that not all legislation adopted by a General Conference, predominantly American in character, can apply effectively in other lands. Hence, the power of making adaptations is given. Some Central Conferences have made such adaptations while others have preferred simply to stay by the *Discipline* of the general church as written.

Other than the responsibility for promoting the work within the Central Conference area the chief power assigned to the Central Conference is the power to elect bishops. This has resulted in time, as it was anticipated that it might, in the election of national leadership to the episcopacy, and the day has now come where every present, active, Central Conference bishop is a native.

The Central Conference system was taken over into The Methodist Church at union in 1939 and into The United Methodist Church in 1968.

In the course of time Central Conferences have developed in India, Southeast Asia, the Philippines, Latin America, Liberia, Africa, Northern Europe, Southern Europe, Germany, and the German Democratic Republic. All these have made strong and lasting contributions to the development of the work in their particular lands.

Autonomous Churches

Just as earlier phases of the administration of the work overseas from the United States have now passed, so the Central Conference system appears in large part to be passing also. The new direction being taken is either that of becoming fully autonomous churches or entering into united churches. Such moves have the blessing of The United Methodist Church if they are what the Central Conference itself favors.

The Central Conference of Southeast Asia has now become a fully autonomous church. The Central Conference of Latin America has been replaced by fully independent Methodist Churches in Argentina, Chile, Bolivia, Peru, Uruguay, and by church unions in Costa Rica and Panama.

The Central Conference of Southern Asia is now moving into union with the Church of North India, and discussions of autonomy are current in the Philippines and Africa. The work in Sierra Leone has become autonomous.

The Central Conferences in Europe appear to favor continuance of the conference system, at least for the present, because being a part of a world church gives to Methodism in Europe a status which it could not enjoy in a situation where numerically it represents so small a minority of people.

As far back as the nineteen twenties the Methodist Episcopal Church, South, began to look with favor upon autonomy for its work overseas, and as early as 1930 it granted autonomy to its largest and strongest field, the work in Brazil. About the same time, it followed the same policy with the work in Mexico as did also the Methodist Episcopal Church.

The Methodist Episcopal Church, the Methodist Episcopal Church, South, the Evangelical Association, and the United Brethren Church all participated gladly in the development of the United Church of Christ in Japan in the 1930s and the organization of the Korean Methodist Church in about the same period.

The Evangelical United Brethren Church in fairly recent years approved merger of its work in the Philippines and in Nigeria into united churches.

The work in Cuba, long a part of the Southeastern Jurisdiction, became autonomous in 1968 and in Costa Rica, Panama, and Sierra Leone in 1972.

All the work originally begun by United Methodism, some in the form of autonomous churches and some in the form of united churches, still goes on. In the economy of God none of the results of it will ever be lost. But the ways of administering the work have of necessity changed with the times. The Central Conference system is but a late chapter in the story, and it too seems largely to be passing in most cases.

The obvious fact is that the portion of United Methodism once thought of as a mission field has become of age. Today is the harvest time of the gospel in these lands. The church there has a trained and able ministerial leadership. It has a strong laity. It has resources of its own and the ability to administer both these and resources that may come to it from elsewhere. It has institutions that now represent some of the truly great educational, healing, and philanthropic institutions of the world, and it has staffing for them. The time has come when these churches should no longer be thought of as receiving churches, but as developed churches and as sending churches. The General Conference and the bishops and the Board of Global Ministries must henceforth deal with them as churches that are now fully grown and with their leadership as one which is mature.

All this is but to suggest that the concept of the Central Conference in United Methodism does not represent one of its basic and probably more abiding concepts. If and when it has served its purpose it too will pass, but the primary idea that lies back of it will continue to have validity, namely the idea that all churches deserve full liberty to develop in their own situation as they feel led of the Holy Spirit.

XV

The Concept of Ecumenism

The United Methodist Church is generally accepted today as an ecumenically minded church, and it has been so
known across the past two centuries. This is not surprising
as those who set it on its course were ecumenically minded
persons. John Wesley was far ahead of most churchmen of
his time in this regard. He sought diligently to learn what
he could from persons of other churches as was evidenced
by his conversations with August Spangenberg of the Moravian colony in Georgia and with Peter Bohler in London
and his visit to Germany shortly after his conversion where
he met and talked with Christian David and Count Zin-
zendorf, head of the Moravian Church. He read diligently
the writings of persons of churches other than his own including Dissenters and Roman Catholics and abridged
and published many of these for the benefit of his followers. His "Letter to a Roman Catholic" and his sermon
on "The Catholic Spirit" are classics of earlier ecumenical
writing. He stated categorically, "I desire a league offen-
sive and defensive with every soldier of Christ," and

154

said to all, "Is thine heart right, as my heart is with thy heart? . . . If it be, give me thine hand." As was common in his day, he did engage at times in theological debate that severely strained relationships, as was the case even with his greatly loved friend, George Whitefield. Nevertheless, he at the same time refused to unchurch in his thinking those who differed from him and maintained a general position of openness toward them and expressed anxiousness to cooperate fully with them in all efforts to extend the gospel.

Philip Otterbein likewise was a man of pronounced ecumenical spirit. No more striking example of this is to be found than in his glad participation in the ordination of Francis Asbury at the Christmas Conference of 1784 and his strong friendly attitude toward and collaboration with the early Methodists. The same cordial attitude which he showed toward these, he showed also toward other evangelical Christians. The very name, "United Brethren," chosen as a result of an unplanned remark upon the occasion of his first meeting with Martin Boehm at Isaac Long's barn in 1767, suggests in itself the genuine catholic spirit of the man and the movement which under God he was instrumental in inaugurating.

Jacob Albright also was a person of the same spirit, having himself crossed denominational lines in his own church membership at least once and leaving behind him a record of leadership in some of the earliest efforts at church union in the United States.

With such an emphasis marking the church fathers it is not to be wondered at that the churches ultimately forming The United Methodist Church have participated fully in ecumenical developments across the last sixty years and have provided for the ecumenical movement such leaders as Frank Mason North, John R. Mott, Eugene R.

Hendrix, Thomas H. Lewis, John S. Stamm, Ivan Lee Holt, G. Bromley Oxnam, James C. Baker in an earlier day, and Reuben H. Mueller, William C. Martin, and Charles C. Parlin in later days.

The United Methodist Church and its predecessor churches have taken the position that an ecumenical spirit should not only represent a general attitude marking the church, but that, much more, it should manifest itself in concrete forms. The forms which United Methodism has chosen by which to manifest the ecumenical spirit have varied across the years.

Fraternal Messengers

Perhaps the oldest manifestation of the ecumenical spirit upon the part of the churches forming The United Methodist Church has been the custom of receiving at the General Conference fraternal delegates from other churches and in turn sending representatives to their representative body. This custom dates far back into history. The story of these fraternal delegate exchanges has never been adequately told. Some of the greatest leaders of the religious world have been called upon to discharge this function, and some of the watersheds in the history of United Methodism have grown out of the appearance and message of some fraternal messenger. Interesting cases in point are: the message of Doctor Thomas H. Lewis of the Methodist Protestant Church to the General Conference of the Methodist Episcopal Church in 1908 in Baltimore which is generally credited with opening the way for Methodist union in 1939; or the message of Bishop Edwin Holt Hughes to the General Conference of the Methodist Episcopal Church, South, in Birmingham in 1938 which won countless friends for union; or the message of

Charles Parlin to the General Conference of the Evangelical United Brethren Church in 1962 which did the same thing. Today fraternal delegates are still received by the General Conference, but the number now invited is so large and the pressure of business is so great that what was once one of the most effective manifestations of the ecumenical spirit has become largely a matter of courtesy and formality.

National Council of Churches

A second manifestation of the ecumenical spirit upon the part of United Methodism has been its continuing identification with the National Council of Churches. The predecessor of the National Council of Churches was the Federal Council of Churches founded in 1908 with a Methodist, Bishop Eugene R. Hendrix of the Methodist Episcopal Church, South, as its first president. At the very beginning the Methodist Episcopal Church, the Methodist Episcopal Church, South, the Methodist Protestant Church, the Evangelical Association, and the United Brethren Church all became members of the council, and their membership has continued without interruption. United Methodists have always been most active in the National Council. Many of them have served and do serve on its staff. The United Methodist Church provides a most substantial part of the council budget and co-operates fully in its multitudinous projects. United Methodist membership in the governing bodies of the National Council is elected by the General Conference or named by the Council of Bishops if the General Conference is not in session at the time nominations are due to be made. These representatives represent a cross section of the church and include church executives, ministers, laymen, laywomen, and youth. The National Council is not a superchurch and has no authority over the churches belonging to it. Rather it is a device by which the churches seek to do together what no one of them could do alone. It carries out numerous cooperative programs and projects which are of significance for the churches and for society as a whole. From time to time it issues pronouncements and policy statements on important social issues. These statements are hammered out after careful and prolonged study and debate and are finally approved by majority vote. They are released to the churches and to the nation for study and consideration. Their only binding force is to be found in the logic of the argument which they present and the persuasiveness of the case they may succeed in making.

World Council of Churches

Another manifestation of the ecumenical spirit of United Methodism is its identification with the World Council of Churches beginning with its organization in Amsterdam in 1948. The World Council functions at the world level in much the same manner as does the National Council on a national level and the relations of The United Methodist Church to it parallel roughly its relations to the National Council. Through the fellowship of the World Council of Churches, The United Methodist Church works cooperatively with over two hundred churches all over the world.

General Conference Representation

Still another manifestation of the interest of The United Methodist Church in ecumenism is found in the plan for seating in the General Conference fraternal delegates from affiliated autonomous churches and affiliated united churches. Originally Methodism operated upon a world church pattern. As work began in various countries it was organized as conferences and representatives of these conferences were present at each General Conference. The same plan was followed in the churches of the Evangelical United Brethren tradition. The period of the nineteen twenties witnessed the rise of independent churches in what had until then been mission fields, particularly in Brazil, Korea, Mexico, and Japan. Some of these were independent Methodist churches, while others were united churches. To maintain some continuing connection with these churches it was provided that each should be invited to send fraternal delegates to be seated in the General Conference with voice but not vote. This practice still continues. Recent years have witnessed accelerated development of independent churches, this with the blessing of the church. Today the United Methodist Church is thus related to some twenty-four independent Methodist Churches or united churches.

World Methodist Council

In 1891 there was held in London what was termed an "ecumenical" conference made up of representatives from the various Methodisms of the world. With this conference what we now know as the World Methodist Council had its beginning. After that, Methodist Ecumenical Conferences were held once every ten years. They were primarily fellowship gatherings highly inspirational in character, and there was little or no formal organization. By 1951 the need for some more formal organization became apparent and the council as we now know it came into being with an executive committee, a staff, headquarters at

Lake Junaluska, North Carolina, and Geneva, Switzerland, and a developing program. The United Methodist Church cooperates fully in this council along with some fifty other Methodist churches in some eighty different countries.

Concordats

Another manifestation of the ecumenical concern of The United Methodist Church is the movement in recent years for the development of concordats. The first of these to be developed is a concordat with the mother church, The Methodist Church of Great Britain which became effective in the British church with the conference of 1970 and in The United Methodist Church with the 1972 General Conference. Under this concordat four delegates from The United Methodist Church, two lay and two clerical, are seated each year in the British Conference, and the same number from the British church are seated in the General Conference. These delegates are full members of the body in each case and are expected to participate freely in discussion and debate and in voting. It is to be expected that in time concordats of similar character may be worked out with affiliated autonomous churches. This would give the advantage to these churches of having voting delegates in the General Conference rather than simply fraternal delegates as they have now and would open their assemblies in turn to voting representation from The United Methodist Church which is not the case at present.

Consultation on Church Union

One of the current evidences of the ecumenical concern of United Methodism is its participation in the Consultation on Church Union. Through this medium nine of the great ecclesiastical bodies of the United States are exploring the possibility of creating a uniting church, truly catholic, truly evangelical, and truly reformed, and in the meantime developing more effective working relationships with each other. United Methodists have given substantial leadership in the consultation, and the General Conference has provided continuing financial support. What the ultimate issue of the consultation may yet prove to be is for the future to determine.

Roman Catholic Relationships

A further evidence of the ecumenical concern of The United Methodist Church is found in new relationships of United Methodism with the Roman Catholic Church in late years. There were United Methodist observers present at Vatican II, and the years since have witnessed formal continuing Methodist-Roman Catholic conversations involving scholarly minds of both churches. Representatives of the Roman Catholic bishops have been heard by the General Conference; Roman Catholic observers have been invited to be present at numerous meetings sponsored by various United Methodist agencies, and at the local level there has been frequent association for fellowship, community service, and worship that would not have been dreamed of only a few years ago.

Continuing Church-to-Church Relationships

In formal relations with other churches and/or ecclesial bodies the Council of Bishops is specified by the *Discipline* as the primary liaison for The United Methodist Church.

Perhaps the most dramatic symbol of the ecumenical spirit of United Methodism is and always has been its fully open communion table. Here all are welcome regardless of creed or baptism or church identification or other religious credentials, if only they love the Lord Jesus Christ in sincerity and "truly and earnestly repent of their sins, and are in love and charity with their neighbors and intend to lead a new life, following the commandments of God and walking henceforth in his holy ways."

XVI

The Concept of the Accomplishment of Mission

United Methodists are not infrequently dubbed activists by certain present-day religious critics. There is a subtle inference in the allegation that they are not sufficiently given to theological formulation, spiritual reflection, precise ritualistic practice, or an obvious concern to be the true church in valid historic succession. This same charge has been leveled against them with more or less frequency all across the years. They readily plead guilty to the charge of activism and see in it not a criticism but a compliment of which they trust they may prove fully worthy.

John Wesley was far more than just an activist, but he was nevertheless an activist,—abundant in good works, tireless in the expenditure of physical, mental, and soul energy—who regularly gave every passing moment something to keep in store. He constantly urged his followers to be activists in the best sense, and they responded with gladness, adopting as something of their battle hymn Charles Wesley's immortal lines

> To serve the present age
> My calling to fulfill;
> O may it all my powers engage
> To *do* my Master's will!

The pioneer leaders of the United Brethren and Evangelicals were given to a similar activism, traveling tirelessly and laboring sacrificially if only as a result thereof lost and needy people might be found and brought to God and believers might be built up in the faith.

It is to be admitted that conceivably religious activism at times may be only activism and nothing more and something of a kind of busy work in which one finds pleasure and even some degree of selfish reward. But an activism that is not sustained by genuine faith is an activism that withers in time and that cannot meet demands for sacrifice. The real danger, however, for most professing churchmen is not that they shall be too active, but that they shall not be active enough.

United Methodism has been active in evangelism, in teaching, in missions, in philanthropy, in healing, and in social reform. So it still continues to be, and in the present day it seeks to discover additional new forms of service by which it may conceivably contribute to the coming of a better world.

Structure for Mission

In its concern to be active in good works United Methodism has always realized that effectiveness in mission requires carefully designed structure for mission, and it has majored upon organization to a degree unmatched in most religious bodies. Its genius for organization has been one of the primary secrets of what effectiveness it has enjoyed.

Several overall observations may be made concerning United Methodist structure for mission as we now have it.

United Methodism's primary concern regarding structure has always been mission. This concern has marked it from the beginning. It has never concerned itself with whether or not a New Testament precedent could be found for a particular feature of its economy, or with the question of how a proposed form might fit in with ancient church order. To some extent it has altered its structure with every General Conference, although the basic pattern has remained largely the same. The current popular talk about structure for mission has no strange sound for United Methodist ears. Rather it represents a concept which United Methodism has always accepted and sought to translate into practice.

Structure Development

United Methodist structure has been a development, a development that covers now almost two centuries. This accounts for certain cumbersome features in the overall structure which we now possess. It is as if a man built a small house in Baltimore in 1784 and then added something to it every four years as he felt led. While on several occasions there have been studies ordered by the General Conference of certain features of United Methodist structure and polity such as the ministry, the episcopacy, or the board composition of the church, our total economy has never been so reviewed as a whole.

It is to be further remembered that each particular

agency of the church has been developed to meet what at the time of its inception was felt to be an ummet need. No agency came into being without strong apparent reason. In some cases the argument was that the particular need at which the proposed agency was beamed was totally unmet and in others that while conceivably it might be met by already existing agencies of the church, actually they were not meeting it, and there appeared at the time little hope that they would.

Local Churches

The primary unit in United Methodism's organization for the accomplishment of mission is the local church. It is here that a conscience must be created regarding mission. It is here that individuals must be trained for mission. It is here that inspiration to mission must be generated. And it is here that those resources of personnel and money must be gathered that are needed in mission. Wesley and Otterbein and Albright's simple classes for the organization of converts have become in United Methodism some forty thousand local congregations, large and small, which represent its basic and strategically placed primary units for the accomplishment of mission.

In addition to its local churches United Methodism has seen fit to develop certain overall general church agencies designed also to contribute effectively to the accomplishment of mission.

The Publishing House

The first of such general church agencies to be developed was the Publishing House. The establishment of the Methodist Publishing House came in 1789 only five years after the Methodist Episcopal Church was formally organized. The reason for its establishment was obvious. Christian literature was greatly needed in the way of periodicals and books and later Sunday school material. Supplying this need was profitable both for the preachers who carried the publications in their saddlebags to sell to the people and for providing pension funds for the church after operational expenses of the House had been paid. The basic reason for creating the Publishing House, however, was not profit, but the advancement of mission. Though the Publishing House today has become big business and may be thought of by some as little more, its primary purpose, from the church's viewpoint, is still mission, and aside from this it has no role as a church institution. The stewardship of the press of United Methodism remains, as it has always been, one of the church's most serious responsibilities and at the same time one of its most commanding opportunities for mission.

Periodicals

The establishment of the several publishing houses of the churches now constituting United Methodism heralded the advent of religious periodicals. Some of these were published by the publishing houses themselves. One of the most important among these for long years was the *Christian Advocate* whose first issue appeared in 1826 and which was in due time to be found in almost every typical Methodist home.

Later regional editions of the *Advocate* made their appearance, all of them authorized by the General Conference, their editors being elected by that body. The Church, South, also had its *Christian Advocate* which enjoyed wide circulation.

The Evangelical Association created the *Christliche Botschafter* in 1835. This was the first German weekly church paper to be published in the United States, and for years it remained highly influential. In the United Brethren Church the first issue of *The Religious Telescope* appeared in December 1834.

The Methodist Protestant Church had two widely popular periodicals, *The Methodist Protestant* and *The Methodist Recorder,* both of which enjoyed a succession of particularly able editors.

In addition to the *Christian Advocate,* the Methodist Publishing House developed other periodicals, designed to serve special needs of the church, including especially literature for the church school. The story of many of these periodicals as they made their appearance, served their function, and in turn gave way to other publications is a fascinating one indeed though a generally little known one.

The story of the publications of the publishing houses of the Evangelical Association and the United Brethren Church bears strong similarities.

In addition to these periodicals of the general church there have been other independent and conference periodicals such as the old New Orleans *Christian Advocate* or Zion's *Herald* which have had wide circulation and far-reaching influence in United Methodism.

The very names of many of these earlier periodicals, such as *Advocate* or *Herald* speak eloquently of the positive positions which they endorsed and the trumpet call which they sounded. They have much to suggest to those in United Methodism today who are charged with exercising the stewardship of the press in as confused a day as our own.

ACCOMPLISHMENT OF MISSION

The Missionary Society

The next general agency for the accomplishment of mission to be developed, in point of time, was what was at first called the Missionary Society. This began in the Methodist Episcopal Church in 1819 and was at first simply a voluntary organization of individuals who were interested in missions and willing to make an annual contribution. Missionary societies were also formed at the Annual Conference level.

The Evangelical Association organized its Missionary Society in 1839. It sponsored home missions from the beginning, as well as work in Canada, and sent its first missionaries to Germany in 1851.

Formal organization of missionary work in the United Brethren Church came in 1853.

In Methodism the Missionary Society gradually developed into a board representing and serving the entire church. Time witnessed the development of a number of bodies more or less missionary in character in addition to the board. Some of these were concerned with foreign missions, some with church extension, and some with home missions. Some represented a certain part of the constituency of the church such as women, young people, or children. This multiplicity of groups within the three Methodist churches were brought together with Methodist union in 1939 into one Board of Missions. This and the Evangelical United Brethren Board of Missions were brought together in one board with the union of 1968. At the General Conference of 1972 in Atlanta the Board of Health and Welfare, and the Commission on Ecumenical Affairs were consolidated with the Board of Missions to form the new Board of Global Ministries which is charged with carrying forward a constructive and greatly diversified program of mission upon a truly worldwide scale.

Christian Education in the Local Church

In historical sequence the next area into which the church moved in the field of structure for mission was Christian education in the local church. As early as Wesley's day in Georgia and the period of Asbury's leadership in American Methodism, there were sporadic attempts at the organization of Sunday schools. Sunday schools at first did not find favor among some Methodists, Evangelicals, or United Brethren.

Beginning in 1827 the Sunday School Union of the Methodist Episcopal Church was formed. The establishment of Sunday schools began to be encouraged, Sunday school literature prepared by editors elected by the General Conference was provided for, and Annual Conferences began to plan for and lay emphasis upon Christian education through the local church. In time Sunday school associations at county, state, national, and international levels came into being. These crossed denominational lines and for long years had tremendous impact.

The first General Conference of the Methodist Episcopal Church, South, encouraged the organization of Sunday schools and provided for a Sunday school paper. The conference of 1854 formally established a Sunday School Society which in turn was succeeded by a Sunday School Committee in 1878 and by a Sunday School Board in 1894.

The Methodist Protestant Church made provision for the production of Sunday school literature beginning in 1878.

The 1835 General Conference of the Evangelical Association inaugurated an effort to organize Sunday schools wherever possible, and the 1855 General Conference formally organized the Sunday School and Tract Society.

The United Brethren General Conference of 1865 organized the Sabbath School Association, and four years later the Board of Sunday School Directors was created to administer Sunday school work.

Changes were made from time to time by all the churches now constituting United Methodism in the form of organization provided at the general church level for the encouragement and guidance of local church Christian education, but the concern of the church to be effective at this point has continued unabated since those first faint efforts now well over a century ago. Leadership responsibility is now lodged with the Division of Education of the Board of Discipleship.

Development of young people's work began in all the churches now constituting United Methodism in the 1890s.

Higher Education

During the period following the Civil War, the Freedmen's Aid Society of the Methodist Episcopal Church was born. One of its purposes was to sponsor educational institutions for blacks, and in doing this it wrote a remarkable record. In due time it was realized that there was need for some overall board of education to counsel with and promote the concerns of these and all other institutions of learning sponsored by the church. Accordingly the Board of Education came into being in the Methodist Episcopal Church in 1864. The Methodist Episcopal Church, South, created such a board in 1894 and the United Brethren Church in 1873. The Evangelical Association began to provide guidance for educational institutions with the General Conference of 1871.

The present-day successor to the responsibilities of these former Boards of Education is the Board of Higher Education and Ministry which now carries not only responsibility for the institutions of higher education and the campus ministry, but also for the training of ordained ministers, the work of the chaplains, training for lay ministers, and the filling of the personnel needs of the church.

A most important additional agency of the church functioning in the field of higher education is the University Senate which is the accrediting and standardizing agency for all the educational institutions related to The United Methodist Church.

Social Concerns

In the former Methodist Church, the Board of Social Concerns and its predecessor agencies the Board of Temperance and the Board of World Peace, were all born as expressions of the church's feeling at particular hours that these issues needed greater attention than they had been receiving. The Board of Social Concerns has now become the Board of Church and Society.

Its assigned function is to create a Christian conscience and to give guidance to the church as it seeks to discharge the responsibility to help create a better society.

Discipleship

The Board of Evangelism and the Commission on Worship have been united with the former Division of the Local Church, the Division of Curriculum Resources, and the Board of the Laity to form the new Board of Discipleship which has responsibility for giving leadership throughout the church in all that is involved in the enlistment and training of disciples.

The present four major program boards are paralleled at the conference level as each Annual Conference may determine and at the local church level as may appear desirable.

Special Agencies

In addition to these program agencies, a church the size of United Methodism needs necessarily certain purely functional agencies. There is first of all the Council on Finance and Administration which recommends budgets and receives, administers, and distributes the various funds of the church. This fiscal operation of United Methodism is by its very nature a large, intricate, and detailed operation.

Agencies of United Methodism rendering other specialized services for the church include the Joint Committee on Communications which serves the Council on Ministries and the general boards and agencies of the church in meeting their communication needs, the Board of Pensions which administers its pension program, and the Commission on Archives and History which assembles and preserves the church's records.

As of the present there are two commissions presumably temporary in nature, as by definition United Methodist commissions always are, as over against a board which is thought of as more or less permanent. These are the Commission of Religion and Race and the Commission on the Status and Role of Women in the Church. These are designed to deal with important pressing concerns on which it is felt by the General Conference that attention now needs to be focused.

Certain overall directives are given in the *Discipline* for those who as members or directors of various general boards and agencies have responsibility for decision-making. Basic members must be elected by either the General Conference itself or by the Jurisdictional Conferences upon nomination of the Annual Conferences as the *Discipline* may specify.

Members-at-large who are named to protect minority interests or to provide needed expertise are to be elected by the agencies themselves according to a prescribed forula. Episcopal members are nominated by the Council of Bishops and elected by the General Conference.

Members, except bishops, can serve on only one agency at a time, and membership in any agency is limited to eight years.

The various agencies as we now know them represent United Methodism's current organization for the accomplishment of mission. As this organization has changed often across the years since 1784, so it may be expected to continue to change in the future, for United Methodists have always been pragmatists. For them workability has long been the test of truth. To them structure is not sacrosanct. They continue to ask what it is that promises to advance further and more quickly the mission of the church, and having reached a conclusion at this point they have not hesitated to alter structure accordingly.

The Council on Ministries

The latest development in United Methodism's organization for the accomplishment of mission is the establishment of the Council on Ministries by the 1972 General Conference.

The proposal for the establishment of a General Council on Ministries was based upon the assumption that the time had come when United Methodism needed an interim body to serve between General Conferences which was representative of the entire church, and was given limited power by the General Conference to deal with ongoing programs and with new situations which might arise between its quadrennial sessions.

The council represents an overall body to which all program agencies have continuing responsibility. One acknowledgement of such is found in the provision for the election of each general secretary by the general Council on Ministries. This revives in a measure what was practiced prior to 1939 in the churches making up the former Methodist Church and prior to 1968 in the former Evangelical United Brethren Church, the election of administrative officers by the entire church in the General Conference. Election by the Council on Ministries, however, is guarded by provision for nomination by the respective agencies so that their proper concerns as to staff are not ignored or overlooked. Another acknowledgement is the duty assigned to the Council on Ministries to review and evaluate the effectiveness of the general program agencies.

Again the Council on Ministries represents a body that possesses power to coordinate programs emerging from the respective agencies thus preventing unnecessary and costly duplication and conflict and which is given responsibility to study ever-changing missional needs, to engage in research and planning, to determine priorities, and under certain conditions to make changes in missional priorities between sessions of the General Conference. It is also authorized to make recommendations to the Council on Finance and Administration relative to financial program support.

The Council on Ministries is so constituted as to guarantee each Annual Conference representation on this important overall, continuing body just as it is assured representation in the General Conference itself. Thus the way is opened for a closer, continuous tie-in between the general church at the board and agency level and the church at the Annual Conference level than was ever obtained before in the life of at least that part of the church coming out of the Methodist tradition. The plan represents nothing new to that part of the church coming out of the Evangelical United Brethren Church for in that church every Annual Conference was represented on the important continuing unit known as the Council on Administration.

Because the Council on Ministries has ad interim certain responsibilities and limited powers assigned to it by the General Conference, its basic membership is elected by the Jurisdictional Conferences from nominations presented by the respective Annual Conferences of persons who were themselves members of the previous General Conference. Thus some measure of continuity with the General Conference is insured. Provision is made in the legislation for a proper balance in membership between clerical persons and lay persons. In addition, provision is made for at-large membership to insure representation for minorities in the church.

Six bishops chosen by the Council of Bishops are members of the Council on Ministries, but are not eligible for the presidency of the council. The general secretaries, as in the case of the General Conference, have voice but not vote. There is provision for having a general secretary for the council and a limited staff.

There may be a Jurisdictional Council on Ministries as each Jurisdictional Conference may determine.

The Council on Ministries at the general church level is parallelled at the Annual Conference level by the Annual Conference Council on Ministries, at the district level by a District Council on Ministries, and at the local church level by the local church Council on Ministries.

Thus provision is made at every level of the church's life for united planning and promotion of program in such a way as to assure efficiency and effectiveness.

XVII

The Concept of Relatedness

The United Methodist Church and its predecessor churches have been instrumental in the establishment of literally hundreds of institutions of various kinds during the past two centuries. These have included schools, colleges, universities, hospitals, homes for children, older people, or working young people, social centers, and in these later days new experimental ministries of sundry character.

A large number of these institutions having served their day and generation well have long since passed out of existence, and their story is now almost altogether forgotten. Others have passed into the hands of local communities or independent corporations, but The United Methodist Church having brought them to birth still, in effect, continues to serve humanity through their ministry to society. Of these hundreds of institutions one hundred forty-one schools, colleges, seminaries, and universities and some three hundred forty-two hospitals and homes in the United States remain officially related to The United

Methodist Church. In addition there are hundreds of other institutions of sundry character in some forty countries outside the United States which stand in some relation to United Methodism through the Central Conferences, the affiliated autonomous churches, and the Board of Global Ministries.

The general term commonly used today to define the relationship of these institutions, particularly to the church within the United States, is "church-related." The question naturally arises therefore as to what this now commonly used term implies.

Ways of Being Related

The Methodist Church in the United States at the time of its organizing conference in 1784 decided to move into the field of institutions by establishing Cokesbury College in Maryland. The institution was short-lived. A few years later certain academies were established including Ebenezer in Virginia, Bethel Academy in Kentucky, and others. Apparently these first institutions were regarded as creatures of the connection, and relationship with them was largely through the bishops. Bishop Asbury seems to have had much to do with decisions regarding property, selection of the faculty, and general operation. It was a day when the church was small and when the mandate for the bishops to oversee the temporal and spiritual affairs of the church was taken, and could be taken, literally. These earliest educational institutions of Methodism had only a brief existence, and for some years thereafter the church gave its attention primarily to evangelism and the establishment of congregations.

In the twenties of the nineteenth century, Methodism began in earnest to establish institutions, particularly educational institutions. This process began in the United Brethren Church in 1854 and in the Evangelical Association in 1853. In due time there were literally scores of such institutions with some manner of church connection. Some of them were privately and individually owned by some member of the conference whose appointment was made to the presidency of the school rather than to a local parish. Some of these ministers maintained schools of unusually high quality, and some were successful in developing them into financially profitable enterprises. Most of these schools, once privately owned by ministers, have long since become only a vague memory, but a few of them still continue as high-quality, privately owned institutions.

Others of these early educational institutions were more or less directly related, particularly to Annual Conferences or groups of Annual Conferences. Over a long period of years in most cases this relationship was generally somewhat loosely defined. In each case what relationship there was was spelled out by the charter of the particular institution. Perhaps the most common pattern of relationship was through some provision that the trustees of the institution should be either elected or confirmed by the church. In some cases provision was also made for the Annual Conference or conferences to name "Boards of Visitors" whose actual function and powers differed greatly in the case of different institutions.

Among the most important educational institutions of the church are its seminaries. These were relatively late in developing, most of them coming into existence after the churches had behind them a hundred years or more of history. In all five churches forming what is now The United Methodist Church, there was strong resistance at first to seminaries upon the part of some who feared that an educated ministry might be a less devoted and fervent ministry. For this reason some of the earlier seminaries were developed apart from any General Conference action and with largely independent boards of trustees. In some cases what were actually intended to be divinity schools were set up as biblical departments of universities. Because of the history involved in their founding the various seminaries of United Methodism are now set up in differing ways. Today Southern Methodist and Emory universities, together with their Schools of Theology, belong respectfully to the South Central and Southeastern jurisdictions. Gammon belongs ultimately to the Board of Higher Education. In the case of the other seminaries title is in the Board of Trustees. In many cases there is charter provision for at least some of the trustees to be elected or confirmed by annual conferences or some other church body. Nevertheless all these institutions for the training of ministers, held in different ways growing out of the situation at the time of their inception, are now properly regarded as being equally the seminaries of the church, and all receive the blessing and financial support of the church.

The middle nineteenth century saw the church moving into the establishment of other types of institutions in addition to schools, particularly homes for children, hospitals, and in due time social centers, hostels, homes for elderly people, and Wesley Foundations. Again the problem of defining relationships had to be faced and in each case written into the charter or bylaws of the particular institution. In many instances as in the case of a number of the colleges this relationship was again somewhat loosely defined.

The *Discipline* now provides an overall directive that sixty percent of all trustees of United Methodist-related institutions shall be members of The United Methodist Church and that all shall be nominated, confirmed, or elected by some governing body of the church.

What Relatedness Implies

The question of what is actually involved in church-relatedness and the extent to which the church actually "owns" its institutions has come to the fore numerous times across the years, and there are today some strong institutions which once had close connection with United Methodism which no longer have any formal connection of any kind with it.

The issue of what is involved in church-relatedness came to the fore dramatically in the case of Vanderbilt University now a half century ago. Vanderbilt had long been the university of the Methodist Episcopal Church, South, and its one divinity school. In a controversy between the administration, the trustees, the bishops, and the General Conference, much of which was unnecessary and all of which is best forgotten, the university was lost to the church in 1914. Finally by a vote of the General Conference which in essence abandoned what control the courts had declared that the church did have, the tie between the church and the university was severed. The Church, South, then proceeded to establish two new universities, Emory University at Atlanta and Southern Methodist University at Dallas. Stringent effort was made to insure that these were fully "owned" and "controlled" by the church.

More recent years have seen upon the part of the church a decreasing emphasis upon the idea of "ownership" of institutions, and especially upon the idea of "control." This is partly because of the broader and more tolerant attitude of present times, and partly because of the difficulty, to say nothing of the impracticality, of being too rigid in defining and attempting to handle such relationships.

There are at least four things that the term "church-related" implies with reference to any church institution. The first is that the church in some way had some part in bringing the institution to birth. The second is that the church under the charter has some voice in the nomination, election, or confirmation of the trustees of the institution. The third is that the church is looked to by the institution for some measure of support. And the fourth is that there is normally a provision that the church has final claim to the property should the institution for any reason cease to exist.

What Relatedness Does Not Imply

What is more difficult for many of our people to understand, however, is what church-relatedness does not imply.

Church-relatedness does not imply the power of the church to tell the trustees of an institution what to do. This holds for an Annual Conference, a Jurisdictional Conference, or even the General Conference. Once the trustees of an institution are properly elected they have full responsibility for the operation of the institution, and the church does not have the power to instruct them. And certainly the bishop of the area in which an institution is located has no such power. It is frequently thought, even by United Methodists, that a bishop can, if he will, determine finally what happens in any institution in his area. But United Methodist bishops have no such power under the law of the church or under the particular charters of United Methodist institutions.

In 1960 in Decision 166 the Judicial Council in the case of an appeal from Southern Methodist University held that "no conference in The Methodist Church has any right, in our opinion, to dictate to the Trustees of the University matters of policy, procedure or administration. In the operation of the University, except as limited by its corporate charter, the Trustees are an autonomous group." The same reasoning would hold of course in the case of trustees of other institutions. Once elected they are fully in charge unless the charter of the institution itself provides otherwise.

Furthermore church-relatedness does not imply the right of a sponsoring church body to ignore the concept of academic freedom in educational institutions; or the freedom of the pulpit in the case of a local church or the freedom of the press in the case of periodicals owned or sponsored by the church. These are concepts accepted by the church as a part of its social thinking and though the exercise of such freedoms may at times involve difficulty and even embarrassment for the church, they must be lived with for the sake of the overwhelming value which freedom itself represents.

The question arises therefore as to how the church may bring its thinking to bear upon the institutions to which it is related.

The first hope is through the administrator of the institution. If he or she is a person who loves the church, respects it, understands it, and is willing to enter into understanding dialogue with its varied constituency most problems growing out of church relationships can find solution. Unfortunately far too many sad chapters in the history of relationships have centered around strong and unyielding and sometimes bitter personalities in both church and institution.

A second way by which the church can bring its mind to bear upon the institutions to which it is related is through its power to nominate, elect, or confirm the trustees. All too often this power is exercised mechanically and without too much thought, although it represents the living link of the church with its institutions. To allow a situation to arise where the only remedy appears to be to vacate a board of trustees is tragic indeed and can result finally even in severed relationships. The vacating of an entire board of trustees would be still more difficult where the terms are staggered and where such vacating therefore would mean expulsion from office rather than simple replacement at the end of an expired term. Better it is to guard well in the beginning the election of trustees and to be sure that they are persons who have at least deep respect for the church as the sponsoring body of the institution.

A third method that is sometimes suggested all too quickly is that of withholding support. This is too simple a remedy and should be resorted to only after the most careful and conscientious consideration of all issues involved and after all other appeals have been exhausted.

The most effective way, however, for the church to bring its mind to bear upon its institutions is through moral suasion by way of its adopted positions and pronouncements, by way of its teaching and preaching, and by way of the personal persuasiveness of its leadership. Trustees, like all other human beings react defensively to pressure, but most of them, like all basically good men, are open to conviction and responsive to sincere persuasion.

XVIII

The Attic of United Methodism

One of the interesting features of many homes is the attic. Here is gathered together a strange, unorganized, fascinating accumulation of things that the family has discarded, some of them for long years. Each one of them has a story behind it, if it were only known. And each of them represents something that was once considered of value and use, but which finally with the passage of time was laid aside. Incidentally there are those who realize that some of these things once treasured and then cast aside still have value and can yet be put to new use in a new day, and the process of renewing the use of what has been long abandoned has become lucrative business for many.

United Methodism, as it were, likewise has an attic wherein are gathered the memories of things that it once cherished, but in due time saw fit for various reasons to lay aside. Some passing review of these abandoned features of United Methodist polity and practice may prove of some interest not merely to those interested in the history of the church or to those who find some pleasure in nostalgic reminiscing, but likewise to those who are concerned that the church shall continue to meet the needs of people and are anxious to find suggestions from any source, whether it be past or present, as to how this may be done effectively.

We turn then to a consideration of some features of earlier church life in the denominations entering into United Methodist union, which for various reasons have been laid aside.

The Class

One of the earliest features of Methodist polity is what was known as the class. Its inception goes back to Wesley himself. As a result of his preaching and that of those who labored with him in the Evangelical Revival, many persons were converted and many already professed Christians were prompted to lead a new life. These he organized into religious societies beginning in 1739. Each society met once a week. For more efficient functioning the society was divided into classes, usually numbering about twelve persons, one of whom was the leader. Every member of society was assigned to a class whose meetings he or she was expected to attend regularly. In the class the closest inquiry was made into each member's state of grace, the closest attention was given to helping each, to use the ancient Methodist term, "go on to perfection." Specific guidelines for the conduct of class members were laid down which have long been known as the General Rules and which still are embodied in the *Discipline*.

Each class member was expected to make a weekly contribution commensurate with his or her ability to give.

The class system begun in English Methodism under

Wesley was carried over into American Methodism in the early days. Two features of it are particularly worth noting. The first is the complete coverage of the class system as originally established. Provision was thereby guaranteed for close "watchcare" of the entire membership. The second is the strong emphasis upon spiritual growth and development, by the provision of guidelines, by the insistence upon continuing soul-searching, by the sharing of experience, and by the stimulation of Christian fellowship.

In due time in Methodism the assignment of every member of the church to some class fell into disuse. An attempt to revive something of such a plan was made early in the present century largely under the leadership of Bishop Frederich T. Keeney through what was known as the Million Unit Fellowship Plan, but this movement was relatively short-lived.

United Methodism in the later years has never had anything that matches the complete "watchcare" of its members that the church had in earlier years. This may have something to suggest with reference to our current inordinate proportion of inactive members and our tragic losses in membership in late years. The class system when it was in full vogue had its losses too, but the proportion was not so high as now, and when a member was lost from the society it was only after the most diligent effort had been made to keep him within the fold, and the reasons for his return to the world were known and sometimes even entered into the record. He did not simply drop out of sight.

As the close assignment of every member to a class began to drop out of use, what was called the class meeting came into vogue. This was usually a weekly meeting for prayer, praise, and testimony, normally under the leadership of a lay person. It did not include all members of the local church, although it was always open for all who desired to do so to attend. Normally it was attended by certain devout souls in every congregation who found strength and inspiration from the informal type of service which it represented. For long years the class meeting remained an important feature of the life of most local churches, but gradually it too began to fall into disuse. The writings of many church leaders, including most of the bishops of fifty to seventy-five years ago lament its evident passing at that time as a sure sign of the lowering of the spiritual level of the church. Today this once prominent feature of our polity remains only a vague memory in the mind of a few older United Methodists.

The Steward

The term "steward" is one of the oldest and most honored to be found in United Methodist polity. It too goes back to Wesley who as early as 1739 provided for stewards in each society. These received and administered the funds of the various societies.

The office of steward in turn became a feature of the polity of the Methodist Church in the United States and continued as such until 1968, the time of union, when almost without notice it passed out of sight. Today the age-honored term "steward" does not appear in the *Discipline* except for the provision for a district steward charged to care for certain routine district fiscal matters.

The steward is now replaced by at-large members of the Administrative Board, who carry many of the responsibilities he once carried.

The traditional steward is worth remembering, however, and United Methodism is forever in his debt. Especially in the days of the circuit system, he made regularly the round of the members assigned to him and collected their gifts for the support of the ministry and the program of the church. Often in small congregations he and perhaps one or two other stewards who served with him literally held the church together. In larger congregations the stewards, organized as a board, looked after the business affairs of the church, developed budgets, raised and distributed funds, and developed plans for the church's response to community and world need.

Originally Methodism asked that the stewards be "men of solid piety who both know and love the Methodist doctrine and discipline and are of good natural and acquired abilities to transact the temporal business of its church." Later this now quaint language was changed to read "persons of genuine Christian character who love the Church, . . . and are competent to administer its affairs." The steward as he was once known is now no more, but The United Methodist Church still asks the same thing of his successors, the members of the Administrative Board, and adds further that they be "morally disciplined, . . . loyal to the ethical standards of The United Methodist Church set forth in . . . the Social Principles."

Love Feasts and Testimony Meetings

One of the earliest developments in the United Methodist tradition was what was called the love feast. It found its inspiration in the love feasts or agapae of the early church in which the first Christians ate and drank together signifying their Christian love for one another. Such fellowship meetings were marked by prayer, singing, and religious conversation and exhortation. Wesley patterned the love feasts after this New Testament practice and provided that they be held quarterly. The elements provided for eating and drinking together were plain bread and water. The love feasts were confined to members in good standing, and admission was by ticket given by the pastor as an indication that the person receiving it had been living as becomes the gospel. Some of these ancient tickets are still the prized possession of the descendents of these faithful forebears of yesterday. In due time the use of tickets was discontinued, and gradually the love feast itself fell into disuse. The time was not too long ago when a love feast was one of the highlights of every Annual Conference session.

Normally the chief feature of the love feast was testimony, and the leader urged those attending to "tell what the Lord had done for them." Those in the United Methodist tradition have always believed that there is great value in Christian testimony both for the person speaking and the person hearing, and in the yesterdays they often urged, "Let the redeemed of the Lord say so." It was a simple step from the love feast to the testimony meeting still common in our churches a half century ago and to the large use of testimony in revival services.

The love feast and the testimony service served their day and generation well and made lasting contributions to countless lives, but in due time they too found their way into the attic of United Methodism.

The Shouting Methodist

A familiar figure once in Methodism was what was long called a "shouting Methodist." Almost every local church once had one or more such devout individuals whose cup would get full occasionally and whose emotions would overflow prompting them to shout out of the ecstasy of their souls. Sometimes they would weep; sometimes they would cry out in happy hallelujahs; sometimes they would sing; and sometimes they would even jump up and down in gladness. This phenomenon was particularly marked in the era of the first camp meetings, but forms of it continued for years thereafter among those in the United Methodist tradition.

Not all Methodists in an earlier day were "shouting Methodists." In fact the majority of them were not this vocal in giving expression to their religious feelings, and many of them looked with some disapproval and questioning upon those who did.

But Methodists and United Brethren and Evangelicals as a whole were a glad people. There was a marked note of joy about their religion which found expression in their prayers, their testimony, and particularly in their songs. All were a singing people. The Wesleyan Revival resulted in a great outburst of song, marked especially by the hymns of Charles Wesley, which before life was over for him came to total some six thousand in all. Other Methodist hymnists have followed in Charles Wesley's train and have given the Christian world some of its great hymns of overflowing Christian experience.

The shouting Methodist, though now only a fast-fading memory, serves to remind us at least of the gladness that has marked us as a people, and that should continue to mark us in a day that so sorely needs the happiness that is born of great faith.

The Exhorter

The exhorter is an almost altogether forgotten figure in United Methodism, but he was an important figure once, especially in the smaller churches. He was a step below the local preacher. The requirements for an exhorter's license were still lower than those for a local preacher's license. The exhorter was subject to an annual passage of his character and renewal of his license. He was not expected to take a text and preach a formal sermon. Rather he was to give what the title of his office implies, an exhortation. Methodism in the age to which he belonged, laid great stress upon the hortatory note. The exhorters were men who were particularly "fervent in spirit." At one time it was customary for them, after the preacher had delivered his sermon, to take over, and with earnest pleas urge evidence of its acceptance by some appropriate action. Particularly did the exhorter call mourners to the altar. At one time the labors of these humble, often unlettered men brought multiplied thousands into the kingdom as with an almost innate knowledge of human response, they practiced with consummate skill the now almost forgotten art of "drawing the net."

The Mourner's Bench and Altar

Recalling the exhorter it is natural to recall also the mourner's bench and altar once so commonly used among those in the United Methodist tradition. These bodies believed that sinners should be called to repentance and to the exercise of faith, and they had their own carefully devised means and techniques to bring this about.

In the tabernacles used in camp meetings they had a crude bench or benches at the front termed the mourners' bench. Some of the early churches also had mourners' benches. In some cases these were regular benches at the front of the church. In others they were a low bench running within the chancel rail of the church where penitents sat or knelt. In most cases the regular chancel or altar of the church served the same purpose.

Once seekers had come forward for prayer in response to the invitation it was the business of the pastor, the lay preacher, the exhorter, and other Christian workers to pray with them and lead them into that repentance and exercise of faith that resulted in the experience of conversion.

Such use of the mourners' bench and the altar as was once commonly practiced is now largely only a fading memory in most United Methodist churches. Certain present adaptations of these ancient methods however are working effectively in numbers of our churches, both large and small.

Camp Meetings

Camp meetings for long years were important features of Methodist and Evangelical United Brethren practice that never officially got into the *Discipline* by way of actual legislation. The first camp meetings came into being beginning around the year 1800. Originally they were meetings in the woods where people came from miles around and camped for days. It is often forgotten that at first they were often called sacramental meetings and that one of their important functions was to make the sacraments available. There was much preaching, praying, singing, testifying, and informal Christian fellowship. Thousands of persons were converted, and sometimes the emotional scenes attending the services were almost beyond description. So successful were these meetings that the bishops urged the establishment of camp meetings everywhere, preferably one for every district. For a hundred years the camp meeting had its day and gathered its harvest, but with the coming of new times and new lifestyles it gradually fell into disuse. Today only a handful of these hundreds of camps yet remain. To some limited extent their place has been taken by conference and district camps particularly for young people and by the great assemblies of our own day such as Lake Junaluska or Mt. Sequoyah or Ocean Grove with their greatly diversified religious programs.

The Protracted Meeting

Somewhat comparable to the camp meeting at the local church level in the churches now forming United Methodism was the revival or as it was often popularly called "the protracted meeting." For well over a century it was customary for such a meeting to be held annually in almost every church. Usually the meeting lasted for at least two weeks, but would be protracted further if the interest ran sufficiently high. Normally services were held at least twice a day, and use was made of special evangelists and of singing talent. Churches of other denominations nearby would often join in, and often an entire community would be greatly stirred. Great crowds would be in attendance, including nonchurch people as well as church people. There would be spirited singing and fervent preaching and altar calls and often many happy conversions. Particularly in many circuit churches the protracted meeting represented the one period of concentration in the entire church year.

Today revivals are still held in many United Methodist churches, but in a new day they are quite different indeed from the protracted meetings of the yesterdays.

195

The Quarterly Conference

For long years the Quarterly Conference represented a pivotol point in church life antecedent to United Methodism as we now know it. It was the time when the presiding elder or superintendent came, representing the connection of the charge with the larger church. Often his visit lasted for several days. The various churches on a charge would come together at one of the churches, and there would be preaching, a love feast, and the serving of holy communion. In addition there would be held the business session when the stewards would bring in "the quarterage" as the money for the support of the ministry was then called. Usually each steward came forward and laid on the table the amount he had collected from the members assigned to him. Other necessary business was conducted by way of the calling of certain questions on a form provided for the use of the presiding elder or superintendent in conducting the business of the Quarterly Conference. The purpose of this form was to insure such uniformity in the Quarterly Conferences, as might naturally be desired in a truly connectional church. Generally these Quarterly Conferences were regarded as occasions to which to look forward, especially in the rural churches, and often they were a ccompanied by "dinner on the grounds" and thus became occasions for happy informal fellowship as well as for worship and business.

With the coming of new times the Quarterly Conference has been replaced by the Charge Conference which is extremely important in a connectional system, but which is now required to be held only annually. The Charge Conference is primarily a business meeting and necessarily has about it less glamour than the earlier Quarterly Conference.

The Sunday School Superintendent

No look at the attic of United Methodism would be complete without at least brief notice of the Sunday school superintendent. For long years his was perhaps the most honored, respected, and visible position in the local church. He was a person in whom the people had confidence and who was known for his devotion and particularly for his love for young people and children. In an earlier day, and for long years in rural situations, he carried almost alone the responsibility for planning and carrying forward the work of the Sunday school. Among other things he presided in what were known as the "opening and closing exercises," and these represented his throne. In this capacity he would insist upon spirited singing, often made a brief talk, and called for the report of the classes as to attendance and offering. Most of these early superintendents were very proud of their schools and worked diligently to make them what they termed a success, both in attendance and program.

Especially was the superintendent of a Sunday school in a rural area proud if the school was what was called an "evergreen Sunday school" which meant that it met all year despite bad roads and inclement weather.

With the acceptance of the graded concept in Christian education, the departmental organization of the Sunday school, and the development of local church commissions on education the Sunday school superintendent himself necessarily became more and more a less conspicuous figure. Today he no longer appears in the *Discipline,* and his place is taken by an optional officer now called the superintendent of study. The Sunday school superintendent, however, remains in memory as a beloved figure and one, the final meaning of whose ministry cannot be assessed until the books of eternity are opened at last.

The Circuit Rider

No figure of United Methodism in the yesterdays is more striking or of greater importance than the circuit rider. It was largely he who made the church as we now know it. Riding his familiar horse without wearying he carried the gospel to the people. His saddlebags were stuffed in part with what little spare clothing he had, but chiefly with Bibles and books and pamphlets to be distributed among the people. He was the embodiment of the circuit system. His circuit at first often embraced as high as thirty to forty preaching places, and it took him a month to six weeks to get around. He literally lived in the homes of the people. As time passed the circuits became smaller in compass and the churches stronger, and a circuit parsonage was provided, but still the circuit rider followed tirelessly his endless rounds.

Today the circuit rider is gone, together with his faithful horse, and the circuit itself has largely disappeared. In the circuit's place are the station churches, the half stations, the larger parishes, and group ministries. And in the place of the circuit preacher is the present-day minister who often with something of the same devotion and love for people covers in a matter of minutes in his car the journey which took the circuit rider long hours.

Other Features

Tarrying yet longer in the attic of United Methodism other features of polity and practice long since passed away may be recalled, some of them specifically provided for in the *Discipline,* and others common but not thus specifically covered in the law of the church.

These might include matters as congregational singing with the hymns lined by the preacher long before there were hymnbooks or choirs or musical instruments. They might include the practice of holding services in homes or under brush arbors. They might include the early insistence upon plainness in church buildings or upon simplicity in dress by our people and the discountenancing of gold and costly apparel. They might include the one-time avoidance of certain amusements in strong aversion to "worldliness" of any and every kind. They might include the story of the strong opposition particularly among the United Brethren and Evangelicals to membership in secret societies. And they might include the custom of periodic fasting and the closing of each year with the observance of watch night.

These and other features that once marked the polity and practice of the churches in the United Methodist tradition have long since had their day and ceased to be. They served their generation well and effectively. Occasionally, in our own day with its emphasis upon experimentation, one of these features is revived or a present-day counterpart for one of them is initiated. But they themselves are gone. Laying them aside was often not without heartache, misgiving, and often struggle for the church. But the fact that they were laid aside is evidence of the continuing willingness of United Methodism to make adjustment as the times and situation may demand and to let the mission and its accomplishment determine policy and practice.

XIX

United Methodist Polity and Practice Tomorrow

It may be expected that in the years ahead United Methodist polity and practice will continue to change even as they have during all the years of the past. Each succeeding General Conference will continue to rewrite the *Discipline* as have all General Conferences in the past. And each succeeding generation of United Methodists may be expected to make certain alterations in accepted practices for churches and church members and develop new practices just as the generations of the yesterdays have done.

All churches change with the passing of the years, even the most conservative of them. But it may be fairly claimed that traditionally none of the churches have, in theory at least, been more open to change than have the churches in the United Methodist tradition. This has been largely due to their continuing pragmatic emphasis upon workability, and their long-time conviction that structure should follow mission. No other church automatically subjects its fundamental law to review and possible unlimited

200

alteration regularly every four years. At times some of the changes which have thus been made have been radical and far-reaching in their effect such as the provision for a delegated General Conference operating under a constitution; the admission of lay persons as members of Annual and General Conferences; the too long awaited granting of laity rights and still later clergy rights to women; and the more recent dismantling of a vast world church with the granting of autonomy to units of the church overseas from the United States who desire it.

It is of some interest to recall how such change has come in United Methodism in the past.

Sometimes it has come as a result of a ground swell of opinion among its people. This happened for instance, in the case of laity rights, in the case of Methodist union in 1939 and Methodist-Evangelical United Brethren union in 1968 and in the case of the recent new recognition given to minorities and youth. There simply seemed to appear throughout the church sometimes across a period of some time a strong feeling that certain things ought to be, and change was effected accordingly.

Again change has come because certain individuals of insight have reached a strong conviction at some point and have begun to lift up a banner for the cause dear to their hearts. In doing so they have captured the attention of others and won their support until finally the sought for change has been written into the law of the church. In some cases the leadership thus given by certain individuals has so spotlighted them that they have been elevated to the episcopacy of the church. Some of the great and dramatic chapters in the history of the church revolve about this individual banner-carrying, and it is devoutly to be hoped that some day it will be told adequately.

Change has come in United Methodism as has already been observed through the exercise of the right of petition upon the part of its people. Strange to say, some of the important features of current United Methodist law actually trace back ultimately to some one petition sent to the secretary of the General Conference by a lone United Methodist petitioner. The lone petition thus received has then commended itself to the judgment of the legislative committee to which it was referred and in turn to the full General Conference and has thus been written into law for the entire church.

Again change has come periodically in United Methodism through the leadership of the bishops. This fact is not always recognized or fully appreciated. Some have thought of the bishops as a body as more or less reactionary and as generally opposed to change. Those who make this charge too glibly are not fully acquainted with the history of the church. There have of course been reactionary bishops, and there have been at least some occasions when it might be wished that the bishops as a body might have acted otherwise than they did, but these occasions have actually been relatively few. Those who know the history of the church know that there have been hours when the bishops as a body have given magnificent leadership in effecting greatly needed change. A striking example is the leadership for change given by the bishops of the Methodist Episcopal Church, South, in the General Conference of 1866, particularly those who were elected to the episcopacy that year. This leadership resulted in a genuinely restructured church and one in position to recover from the almost total depletion brought about by the just closed Civil War. Many examples of personal episcopal leadership for change could readily be cited by reference to certain bishops of more recent years such as

Bishops Herbert Welch, Francis J. McConnell, and Edwin Holt Hughes of the Methodist Episcopal Church, or Bishops Eugene R. Hendrix, Edwin D. Mouzon, and John M. Moore of the Methodist Episcopal Church, South, or Bishops James H. Straughn and John C. Broomfield of the Methodist Protestant Church, or Bishops Arthur R. Clippinger, John S. Stamm, and Reuben H. Mueller of the Evangelical United Brethren Church.

In addition the bishops have spoken to the church quadrennially through the episcopal address. There have been few episcopal addresses in now almost two centuries that at some point have not suggested change in the law, the operation, the practices, and the attitudes of the church.

In more recent years some changes have come in the law of the church as a result of the work of study commissions appointed by one General Conference and reporting to the next. These have been given certain features of church polity to review, evaluate, and, if they see fit, suggest changing. All these have done their work with diligence and great care and submitted their recommendations to General Conference for consideration. Some of these recommendations have been approved by General Conference and found their way into law while, of course, others have not.

Of more recent date in United Methodism, as in society as a whole, there has come the appearance of the caucus made up of individuals who have common concerns and who seek to bring group pressure in favor of that which they advocate. The effect of such caucuses is already being felt in the writing of legislation for the church and in elections, though the caucus movement is quite young as yet. The development of one caucus tends, of course, to encourage the organization of other caucuses with similar or contrary objectives.

In addition to what has been said it needs to be observed too, that change has come also in the church, to a very large measure because of the pressure of time and events, for the church continually lives against the backdrop of current history.

The same forces that have operated for change in United Methodism will doubtlessly continue so to operate in the future, and in all probability still other forces will make their appearance.

In the days ahead, perhaps even more than in the yesterdays, the church will continue to find itself living with change and facing the need for further alterations of its structure and patterns of operation.

In such a situation it will need to face whatever need for alteration in polity and practice may arise with wisdom, understanding, and creative imagination.

Valuable guidelines for United Methodism of the future as it lives with change may be found in the telling admonition of Paul in his First Letter to the Thessalonians, "Prove all things; hold fast that which is good." By implication there is a suggestion here that there are some things in life which in time properly should be laid aside in that they have served their purpose and lost their usefulness. On the other hand there is here also the positive suggestion that there are other things in life that should be held on to, despite the fact that they are old and long familiar. The imperative therefore, is to evaluate all things for what they actually may be worth and then to hold fast to that which is good.

The demand resting upon United Methodism in the future, as in the past, is to maintain a proper balance of thinking with reference to its polity and practice. It should on the one hand not hesitate to lay aside whatever of its polity or practice may have lost its value whatever store was once laid by it. It should on the other hand without apology hold fast to those features of its polity and practice which have proved and continue to prove workable and effective which have come down to us as the heritage of our fathers.